THE HAPPY CASTLE

AMERICA & ACTING

james d. wilson

Copyrighted Material

Happy Castle Acting & America

Copyright © 2018 by Makin' A Hand Publishing. All Rights Reserved.

No part of this publication may be reproduced, stored in a retrieval system or transmitted, in any form or by any means—electronic, mechanical, photocopying, recording or otherwise—without prior written permission from the publisher, except for the inclusion of brief quotations in a review.

For information about this title or to order other books and/or electronic media, contact the publisher:
Makin' A Hand Publishing
prairie1943@gmail.com

ISBN: 978-0-9861583-1-5

Printed in the United States of America

Cover and Interior design: 1106 Design

Dedication

Yes.

Also by James D. Wilson

The Man Book: If You're Interested in Being a Man…

Fore-words

I live in north central Wyoming. Rural. That means a whole lotta nature….so

To Baldy and Jack—

I'm still listening,
Still seeing.
Thanks.

Baldy's a mountain. Jack's a rabbit
&
Conversations with-in nature are part of the package here. Takes time to learn the language
because
You have to be still and tune in, into the silence, into the stillness….and learn to wait and to see what's actual….

because
as I understand living
that's how discoveries occur
how self-collisions occur

> how growth happens
> and, therefore,
> how the art of love in living
>
> is born to all of us.

Anyway, in and out of all of that I'm gonna write this: a book....

It begins with....

A decision I made fifty years ago—
University of Minnesota. Summer School—
Just before a mid-August graduation—
Living above Campus Pizza with Stan....

....one hot afternoon, after exploring the couch with a big Czech girl who worked at a bookstore down the street, I stood, staring out the window while she curiously watched me....and I decided and said, 'I want to be one of the best actors who ever lived and I need to go to the opening night party at The Guthrie Theatre'. So....

I went, found Sir Tyrone Guthrie, a very tall, dignified man, pulled on his suit sleeve, and stammered. He said, "Deah boy, once it's cleah to you what you're trying to say to me, come back and speak again."

In a corner of the room, I worked it out and returned. He noticed me and waited, slightly amused. I said, "I want to study at The Central School of Speech and Drama in London. This fall. Will you audition me and if you see enough talent, would you write a letter for me?"

I'd worked as an extra at the Guthrie Theatre and sat in on his private rehearsals. He knew of me. He smiled and said, "That won't be neces'sry. I know the head of the school and I'll be glad to write on your behalf. How are you financially?"

"Poor."

"Good. Let me see what I can do about a McKnight Fellowship."

There's more to this wonderful story. It entails risk, hardship, struggling, thrilling, Ireland and his home, and pursuing my first dream.

Since then, it's been a long career of studying, learning, more dreams, and trying to figure out how to think more accurately, love more fully, teach more effectively, and write the best, most honestly accurate sentences I can.

....a tangent; bear with me:

Life's a word no one can fully define, analyze, or explain.

That means

Life is an actuality and it's our potential. We're in that potential….we call it living.

Living is our glimpse of life.

Living asks us to match life by making *living* as beautiful as we can. That's not easy.

The basic union of life and living is the wild ride we casually call *time*—

> Some of us lose track of time.
> Some of us aren't on time, timely.
> Some us never find the time.
> Some of us never make the time.
> Some us try and try hard....
> Some of us try here and there....
> Some of us quit and walk away.

Some take the full ride, the wild one; we call those folks great persons.

The wild ride includes it all: sun, starry starry night, and darkness—everything that is time....right till the end of our clock time.

Irrespective of the kind of rides we take and make, we all encounter truths that can tell us where we need to go and what we need to do. If we refuse to go where truths lead and we don't believe in hitching rides with truths, then we can easily think and believe we're not hitchhikers; so we end up bereft of some vital truths while standing at roadside, trying to find ways to feel better about not having taken the rides when the time was right.

That implies....

How we think and live is always a mix of more and less light, more and less night, pain, fear, anxiety, some love, some stupidity and stubbornness, regrets, and the presence of 'stars' we call our dreams.

When there are few or no stars in our world and little sun in our days, we're in descent away from light....into a slow crowdedness of nothingness: it's called giving up....starting to die. That kind of dying can occur without knowing it.

Therefore, take the rides, take the time, take time.

That said....

We all think our presence matters a lot or very little, that we're all very small and yet somehow great, or we think/feel we're unhappy and say what's the point, why try so hard when living seems to boil down to bills, a job, worries, money, kids, crime, questions, illness, disease, surgery, loneliness, some fun, longing, waiting, the whatevers, regrets, wondering, sex, food, trying, clothes, watching, buying, struggling, dreaming, aging, and dying.

Living can so often seem that way until we experience moments of pure love.

We all know love can't be defined, analyzed, or explained very well but when it happens we know it, and we feel godlike because we are.

Therefore, two main facts:

Love is why we're alive.

If you don't find love in self and share it *somehow*, you miss out.

This book is partly about all of that and, as stated....

it's about the challenge to live and love
it's about living and loving *in America*
it's about The Modern American Actor/Actress—TMAA....

    &

it's about acting....

If any of that interests you, rock on, read on....

Today In Wyoming Is

February. 5 degrees. Fresh snow. The high will hit 6.

Did a lot of shoveling this week. Be glad when winter throws in the towel.

Baldy is smooth and white at about 10,000 feet. Jack's under tin near the garage.

I was born in Wyoming; grew up 70 miles away. Returned a few years ago to climb another dream....

Moved from L.A. where I taught, taught, taught—taught and coached students, working actors, some stars, myself, and my daughters.

Learned a lot.

Still do.

One day not long ago, I decided to write this book the same way I taught/teach and try to live—that means do the best I can.

Was I an 'acting teacher'? Yes. But most of the time I was a thrilled father and a younger man grappling with ignorance in every area of living—

I knew acting is only part of the big picture called the human situation occurring on a big ball called earth turning in space called existence no one can explain.

I knew the human situation is personal, psychological, cultural, global, spiritual, ontological, cosmological, and symbolical in all ways of diversity, complexity, creativity, and simplicity. I sensed all of that but was unable to articulate any of it.

&

I also knew if students isolated acting into a 'thing' to be pursued and conquered for recognition only, it wouldn't work fully

Because to act fully means to appreciate the fullness of humanness great acting reveals.

I tried to help students sense that and help 'em know that the American version of living and acting occurs in the tangles and angles of democracy, religion, productivity, entertainment, money, and all kinds of fluent and affluent craziness, and in the in poverty and impoverishment that denote how Americans have shaped living into a nation-identity as part of an effort to sleep on stars, ride the sun, and run with gods like little kids....seeking, howling, prowling, and trying to win a yes into the belief that there really is a way to be over the rainbow.

I tried to include enough of the human situation stuff to enhance appreciation for the littlest and the biggest contexts that make us who we are, what we become, and how....while we dangle from the whys, make up answers, make money, laughter and a little love, and try to balance it all into the eventual perception of how quickly years seem to come and go.

I tried to teach students that without courageous awareness and the willingness to develop appreciative knowingness rooted in honesty of thought and effort, it's impossible for anyone in any field to express living for as great as it is, as ugly as it is, as frail as it is, and as beautiful as it can be when it's done right—responsibly in relation to self, self-honesty, truth, change, beauty, and the thrill of learning how to cause happiness for self and others.

Those hundreds and hundreds of students believed they wanted to be actors. I never questioned that or taught anyone differently. Gave 100% while trying to figure out what I didn't know and how to be a more complete teacher. Still do that.

Therefore:

- I tried to let it be known that:
  To be an actor/actress requires deep respect for portrayal rather than emphasis on performance.... that there can be artistry or there will be craft.

That took the study of acting more essentially into the honesty zone: no tricks, no slick, no superficial, no imitation. It slowed their roll a little sometimes, made 'em pause and check in more, or out.

- I tried to convey that:
  Portrayal is complete,
  Performance tries to imitate portrayal,
      and
  Portrayal tends to elude actors/actresses today because of what acting is becoming in America.

Portrayal is a key word for understanding all art, all chosen pursuits, and all education because all genuine creativity in any field produces profiles of practice as portraits of essences.

So....

How I teach/taught/coached and live has always been based on what has to be *learned*—experienced—and *done* authentically: without wasted time, resistance, or confusion.

Call it spare, lean, luxuriously ascetic, out there, irrelevant, too hard, or old school devotion to quality and completeness.

I call it exciting, deeply demanding, and long-term.

There's a price to pay for growth. But growth is worth it.

That tells you I believe:

Learning efficiently and effectively for more learning is all that ultimately counts—through good food, laughter, and love's love in spirit and flesh: the pleasures and joys of the sexual, family and friends, rollercoaster creativity, music, hitchhiking with truths, and jolts of joy that put us on a mountaintop singing a happy song.

That's what continued growth leads to.

Otherwise, you just move horizontally or laterally without much growth and easily develop spiritual tumors that can weigh a lot.

So:

I'm out here on the prairie where Baldy tells it like it is from on high and Jack the Rabbit tells it like it is on the ground.

I've had to listen and look, or leave. I chose to stay.

Each morning I get to open my eyes and take a light-ride, usually on sun.

I take all the rides of the seasons; I ride, then fall off into this cabin at night where I stare at a big star.

What do I ride?

I ride questions. Always have. Saddled up every day since I was a kid. Kept riding till exhaustion, confusion, mistakes, defeat, regret, discouragement, and pain got together and talked to me about naming the reins left and right: what's to be left alone and what's right. And to keep going, seeking, healing, growing, and asking more questions.

To be really clear:

This book is about acting and living and loving in America as you and me because of how we think and how we *act* our 'who' into mattering so we can feel we matter—feel *alive*.

It's about truly true dreams to be actualized through timely action related to accurate personal purpose.

It's about how Americans seek intimacy and belongingness.

It's about great art, The Modern American Actor, students, and The Happy Castle.

Is this book a 'how to' book?
Yes and no.

How to do what?

How to take a fresh look at self, living and loving, acting, and how America handles the ride.

So….this book has its…

LITTLE STRUCTURE:

Nuts and bolts, on the ground actuals derived from

THE BIG STRUCTURE:

The ontological
The real
The contextual
The actual
The potential
    &
The local known as

You, me, the sun of play, and *The Happy Castle*.

That means this book has to be about the most dynamic American Metaphor:

Look Who I Get To Be
&
Look What I Get To Do

Which magically equal the possible.

And that means this book has a whole bunch of...

Loose Contents

- Still Standing or Standing Still?
- Grow Wings With Feathers
- Living Without Tattoos: Missing The Marks
- Secular holiness
- Manhood
- Sincerity & Seriousness
- Seeking Ignorance
- Embracing Inconvenience
- Children Are Not Pennies
- Drama, drama, and melodrama
- The Essence of Cool
- How To Find the 'I' From The 'Eye'
- Brain Theatre and The Lens
- Being On Time For Being
- Laughter & Play: The Truest Genesis
- Habits Rule
- Slick Honey, Blackjack Crown
- Animals Don't Squint
- From What To A Who

- Humility: Belly-crawling A Log High Above A River
- The Greatest Invention: A Mirror For Honest Reflection
- Molding & Molting
- Learning To Work For Air
- The American Actress
- *Great* Person, Great *Person*
- African-American Creativity
- Marry Life Or Marriage is Impossible
- The American Actor
- Naked
- The Body Is An Altar & A Weapon
- Student Acting
- Kids
- Love….River or Faucet?
- Avoid Becoming Your Own Souvenir
- Maturity
- The Weight of Wind….

    And it has….

MORE SPECIFIC CONTENTS

Centered on:

Simplicity
Relevancy
Accuracy
Practicality
&
Facts
That become….

Exact Contents

Fore-words v
Introduction 1
Nuts & Bolts. 3
How Modern American Acting Began 53
American Acting Today. 71
America & The Acting Student 109
Homage To African-American Creativity 165
What's Going On & What's Next 173
Jack. 221
Postscript 235

Introduction

This book properly starts here....

Point A: curiosity-on-the-go, all the way to
Point B: The End.

Just like living.

So who am I?...

I'm an older, on time Pa, G-pa and Papa, man, seeker, lover, laugher, doer, dreamer, and an ex-professor now called Emeritus. I'm playing cowboy again while living solo with an Akita in a little, hundred-year-old cabin perched on a bald knoll that's part of 35 acres in a wide valley climbing the western slopes of mountains in northern Wyoming.

I've planted 33 trees.
I travel 140 miles roundtrip for good groceries.
I haul my own drinking water.

Nuts & Bolts

The First Premise of this book is:

All humans are actors. Some just get paid for it.

The well-known American ones are the gods and goddesses of

> *American secular holiness.*

They help America shape, protect, and protract identity, dreams, values, delights, beliefs, and roles.

They're in our lives

&

They're the central symbol of this book because they're a cultural phenomenon of global significance. Collectively, they are

> *The Modern American Actor....*

TMAA.
Male and female.

American nuts and bolts entail:
Life-altering dreams and screams
Reasoning and its deformities
I from the eye & The Lens
Drama, drama, and melodrama
Slick Honey & Blackjack Crown
Seasons, aging, raging, and denial
Struggling, and standing naked in plain sight and light and no light
    &
The peculiar American treasure hunt for *something* holy.

A word about 'something holy':
Most obviously, that 'something' holy is *kids, the children, the wee ones.*

Americans tend not to see that fully, see how the little ones *live* the miracle of living in spite of us, live it in their play-curiosity-wonder-march every day. And even though they can't know the miracle they're living, they live it as the birth of love so honestly that we who deeply see and appreciate them always feel that same birth *again,* through them.

We learn we can't live without the beauty of children or the holiness of how genuinely they seek and play and see and talk; and if we're receptive, they teach us what we need to learn about the wars in us, the wars of the stars in us, and what to do about making more light.

Children can do that for us and in us without words.

So:

The best response to an invitation from a child is courage. The synonym for courage is giving wisely and consistently.

The worst response is neglect.

The middle ground between giving and neglect is to argue and hurt the kids.

Consider:

If you become a 'non-kid'—someone who doesn't enjoy playing—you'll slide toward boredom and boring.

If you become a non-kid, you age prematurely and immaturely. You slowly stunt....get smaller on the inside....call it a spiritual shrivel

Because....

Non-kiddism always produces too much intellectual seriousness, too much cynicism, too much cognitive emphases, too much competitiveness, too much 'serious' art minus the art, too much thought disorder, too much self-waste, too much control, too much distortion and deformity of desire and reasoning, too much pretentiousness and irresponsible role-playing, and not enough authentic delight rooted in goodness that does not cheapen living or others in any way.

Consider:

Play is the *now* for the *possible*.

It's called creativity—the magical intimacy of making time. That's the genius of being human.

Genius isn't what a person 'is'—'he or she's a genius and I'm dumber'. Doesn't work that way.

Genius is fully accurate effort, purely balanced and sustained. Each of us carry genius potential. We see it even in the wee ones. Genius can make creative thrills that eventually move mountains of doubt and resistance by revealing the essence and power of beauty as truth. But genius requires patient, consistent nurturing or it remains confined to potential.

Kid facts:

- *Non-kids* rule the planet in homes, business, and government. Erroneously, we often call them fathers, mothers, leaders, men, and women.
- *Prominent Playground Kids*—TMAA—are America's dominant cultural 'heroes'. They

entertain us, please us. If they're really fam___, they get to do and have everything, and they don't have to die except away from living.... plus, they get to live in The Happy Castle.... because they're somehow 'special'.

Less well-known Playground Kids are the wonderful scientists, physicians, engineers, leaders, researchers, entrepreneurs, lawyers, philanthropists, volunteers, thinkers, activists, environmentalists, caregivers, memorable teachers, nurses, mommies and papas, animal lovers and helpers, and the thousands of other artists who advance and decorate our culture with their play, photography, paintings, generosity, sculptures, buildings, landscapes, clothing, dancing, laughter, songs, music, and words.

- *Playground Kids* who really go the distance see beyond personal play into love-play: we call them great.
- *Halfway Playground Kids* are productive but they play alone too much and feel it.
- *Negative Playground Kids* end up without playmates.
- *Non-playground Kids* mostly just criticize.

Moving right along:

Yes, America's Premiere Cultural Playground Kids are The Modern American Actor, and many of them live adored for awhile in The Happy Castle.

However....

With The Castle comes the moat....in which floats Castle sewage. We see and hear about that once in awhile.

Consider....

Conventional religion in America is lost among its ruins. It is becoming an expanded, outdated identity reference. A habit.

But American *religiosity* remains a powerful dynamic in American culture—there's a deep, available goodness in Americans.

That said....

Concerts, films, television series, sports events, and award ceremonies, etc., are *not* outdated.

They're the vital sanctuaries, the places where the gods and goddesses perform magic just the way we like it: alive, as in a good time, a connection, a belongingness, a unity, a respite, and a renewal of reunion.

Even though most of us can't live in The Castle, we *can* media-mingle and develop a sense of distant closeness that feels like a kind of actual intimacy because of how we selectively *care* about TMAA without being responsible to or for them.

We can choose who we like and who we want to keep as favorites....

We can get autographs, imitate their clothing, fashions, songs, attitudes, and styles....

We can read about them, talk about them, maybe meet a few, and thank them with our anonymous devotion, interviews, praise, awards, and *dollars*.

Up to this point, the implications of what I've written suggest....

This book has to be about being a human and an American:

....the heaven and hell of consciousness, living and dying, the beauties, the frenzied grandness of America, cultural compulsions and addictions, entertainment, American entitlement and immaturity, the scarcity of joyfulness, sociological myths and rituals, and human stubbornness related to fully accepting responsibilities and invitations to dance, laugh, sing, love, play, and be kind *in spite of pain,* suffering, disappointment, defeat,

The Happy Castle

failure, and the fact that we all will die as anonymously as pebbles in the wilderness.

So....

In greater complex-ification, this book's about dignity, morality, and spiritual maturation; it's about sincere and serious, and about the American Way as *the* most luminous culture on the planet.

That means this nation will stay married to itself as a version/vision of rightness with hierarchical structures bound by the throbbing influences of Judaism and by a sentimental, often defensively static version of Christianity.

All of that gets mixed in and up with deformed democracy in a profile of rebellion, arrogance, chronic negligence, profound conformity, paternalism, self-righteousness, violence, amazing talent and ambition, pathological bias, guns, a lotta beautiful land, that deep goodness, and....*entertainment*.

We can call all that the nuts and bolts of who we are and what we do as 'daily living'....into and through the multiple lenses of technology.

With that in mind, consider:

If you can think of acting as an inherent aspect of human behavior/nature, then what acting signifies more deeply is valid: how we all relate *symbolically* to others through major or minor comparisons, adopted roles and desired roles, appearances, judgments, labels, behaviors, possessions, gestures, feelings, private thoughts, longings, wishes, dreams, and, most importantly....words.

To reiterate:

All humans are actors.
All humans perform roles.
Role-playing is naturally human.

The most intimate role is self.
The most neglected role is self.

The most difficult role to master is self—often due to ignorance, degrees of self-misperception followed by actions of self-deception, limited educational opportunities, and negative stubbornness related to self-alteration.

Facts:

✦ Growth for humans means to experience the activity of matter to *mattering:* the shift from a 'what to an authentic who', then doing your who all the way to the end.

And that, for all of us, means honoring the *motion of meanings* that are in us to move us to move the meanings of living into living by *living* them

- Meanings are all we basically have, so they are all we basically are. They produced our language. That language makes us human and spirit.

I've learned:

- The *motion of meanings*—the potential beauty in each of us—is the essence of our being and therefore of our creativity, the 'urges' that impel us to do something, to enjoy, to make something happen, to discover power in contrast to force.... and then to express our power somehow in some form that shares the meanings.

- Force is physical....related to natural action. Power is spiritual....related to meaningful action, the good.

- Spirit in action is beauty. It opens us to what we are and it helps us open others—namely, the child—to beauty through touch, sight, sound, taste, music, language, affection, guidance, food, and play.

- Trees and animals don't have a problem with love or affection because animals don't squint and trees already have roots.

+ Most humans tend to miss out on full 'growth'. This occurs because aspects of living, mixed with confused thinking and weak actions, can be discouraging. So sometimes it's easier to coast-roll in the same 'ol same 'ol than it is to learn the importance of taking risk-rides from narrow space to wider space....to see better, think better, do better, and love more.
Share.
Grow.

+ Ultimate context is the *big picture:* widest open *space*. All of it. That includes every *little picture* and what we all go through till we die.

That means....narrow space is where we live in altered versions of diminished wide open space. That narrowness of space and our preferred versions of it is what we call our 'personal reality'.

And that's the basis for all distorted thinking: actuality deformed.

+ *Widest open space* is....existence: the pure actuality of all.

That makes existence quite a word. Just like one is also quite a word.
And I. And you.

So, to reiterate....

Most of the time, the contexts of wide open and narrow clash in us because of how we think, feel, fear, and then bulldoze—deny—what we don't like so we can remain in our narrow spaces of preference, opinions, bias, belief habits, fears, and thinking patterns....while pushing for what we want....then pushing others, sometimes around.

+ Keeping it real is different than keeping it actual....

Takes a whole lotta insight, simplicity, kindness, and courage to find actual and embrace it with action....

+ True facts can't be bulldozed no matter how we use language, logic, preference or assumptions, bias, money, denial, force, and conclusions

Because
in the end, our narrow space—personal reality—yields to wide open space....the actual always wins....
We die.

Consider:

+ At birth, we move from a narrow, receptive context (womb) into a widening context of volition that, hopefully, is guided well so we progress, *grow* rather than simply develop—learn how to self-relate effectively and meaningfully, then with others, and, finally, with our potential.

✦ We go from womb to no womb then *into* the first great big magical space called *language*.

Language takes time—a lifetime—to grow into, but early on, language helps prep us more fully for entering the external environment-world with a self-world that is 'centered' and steady, filled with enough wonderful psychological content so 'personality' and true facts can become buddies on a big open stretch of time where meanings and magic and action can mingle productively, pleasurably, and enduringly as a creative self in relationships known as the personal, the interpersonal, the environmental, and the universal. If any of those four aspects of human living are left out or severely diminished, the word spiritual is profoundly curtailed, confined by outdated thinking and *habits*.

✦ That means we cannot fully move/grow into and through each passing decade into the Wide Open Space of time's big picture: the experiences of the big questions that have to be asked and somehow answered to avoid feeling trapped in narrowness by anxiety, personalized reality, and further idiosyncratic/pathological interpretations of space, place, and face.

It's obvious....

+ That it takes a long time to sense the scope of the bigger picture.

But when the bigger picture is sensed and responded to courageously, it's easier for meanings, being, others, beauty, and *strength of self* to be coordinated more continuously for balances and for the discoveries of more *personal integrity*—self-cohesion in continuity and in relationships that are truly good.

+ Integrity always loosens a human into thrills and drills that lead to a mature desire *to give and to teach*....something.

That's ultimately how we grow—through our *thrust* of self into living and giving. It's a process we all go through with greater or lesser ease, interest, and completion.

And....

When it happens, when we do grow, we hit the core of what the word religion most actually is: it's always about all forms of love

Because

If authentic love is made, done, and completed over and over, it becomes the all-embracing context within which all other contexts of existence can be seen to intersect, unite, and gather ultimate aim.

If all effort is aimed at valid love, then growth and creativity can and will be maximized within an evolving experience of self-fulfillment that, as stated, includes generosity, some form of philanthropy, and teaching the young.

- ✦ There's a word in English (when taken off leash, refreshed, and bathed to remove stubborn bias and the manure of culturally distorted rigidities) that is the western symbol for all love, growth, creativity, and maturity.

The word is God....how the nuts and bolts fit together actually.

More on the nuts & bolts of America:

America is a Neon Nation between oceans in the northern hemisphere of Planet Earth turning anonymously in space—

America is land.
America is map.
America is people.
America is culture.
America is a society.
America is its symbols.

America is Slick Honey, Black Jack Crown.
America is Suck Up Your Luck and Don't Back Down
&
America is fiction.
America is driven.
America is play.
America is the global leader.
America is ambivalently spiritual.
America is less interested in history.
America is gutter, struggle, and magic
&
America is a culturally magnetic trance with lotsa applicants here and abroad who dream about some kind of residency in The Happy Castle.

All of that means:

+ The American World of the American Way causes huge creativity, confusion, mismanagement, uncertainty, and a Cultural DUI Predicament defined as frenzy that's basically oriented toward the good, the fun, the dollar, winning in and out of Moses and The Christ, and finding ways to feel cool then special—mattering in American terms.

- America is grand, great, multidimensional, young, a champion, a drunk, a reason, a means, a naivete, a womb, a dream-maker, a don't mess with me pitbull, a compulsion to win, an off-balance, an arrogant, an uptight, a lost, a pathology, a constant erection, an addict, a killer, an anger resentfully denying the superiority of the female, a beauty, a goodness, a steamroller rollercoaster, and the Playground Capitol Of The World.

- America *is* The Happy Castle. And in it live TMAA, the gods and goddesses of fantasy, fun, and *profit*.

They are the idealized versions of The American Wows that are the core of The American Fascinations that drive the commerce of this nation's dreams and its dreamers—us.

So:

Americans hear voices.
Americans seek voices
    &
Americans live primarily in imagination, recreation, calculated effort, emulations, and *pursuits* enhanced by The Dollar & The Lens.

Side note:

I recently asked Baldy, 'What is each day's primary challenge?' Baldy answered, 'Most folks don't ask a mountain a question. Doesn't make sense to do that. And most folks don't live near a mountain that talks. I don't have your problems. I just don't get to move. But I do dream. And talk to clouds. I see your cabin all the time. See you. Each day's primary challenge? The answer is each day. Nice talking to you, Jim'. That's all Baldy said.

The Second Premise of this book is:

The Modern American Actor is *irreplaceable*....
Without TMAA, America would collapse.

That means:

If The Modern American Actor is understood symbolically, contextually, and actual-istically as a comprehensive resource for the continuity of cherished cultural and personal convictions and *needs,* then what I'm writing might make some sense.

Consider:

The Modern American Actor provides an opportunity for millions of Americans to participate vicariously in the continuity of

> The American Versions of Values
> &
> The American Versions of Morality and Love.

That means....

✦ The Modern American Actor is the only deep resource easily available for sustaining and reinforcing American culture.

Churches, temples, and most neighborhoods and communities are, by contrast, relatively weak when compared to the stature of show business and its daily influences on the nation.

The Modern American Actor is a vital part of daily living unless you're a brain-hermit, a latent misanthropist, or a budding cynic mired in extreme denial and angry self-wastefulness. Unfortunately, cynics take the true meaning of pornography to another level, and they learn to *enjoy* loveless-ness as though it's good.

Moving right along....

A few more facts:

+ Any failure to engage with perfections—the 'beautifuls'—is the basis for nearly all explanations of human suffering, fear, and anxiety.

+ Not to look for and affirm the beautifuls through action is to stand at the edge of the dance floor enviously, and become a watcher, a talker. Passive. Then critical. Resentful. This is the onset of becoming a potato.

+ Wisdom is always love-oriented and action-driven.

Dreamers know this.
Authentic actors/actresses know this.
And....

Really good actors/ actresses also know:

+ The less one is willing to know, the less is one's courage and capacity for loving and better acting.

+ The less one is willing to learn and love, the less is one's capacity for truth and better acting.

+ All true artists in any field know love and truth are ultimately derived from reception through giving, participating, and making....but not through control.

Yet, so often in America, artistry is shaped by the need to control....to somehow feel American Strong *and* artistic—a winner—then sustain both.

About that....

Being 'strong' is a dominant influence in American perspectives and, therefore, in American acting.

That kind of 'strong' is different than the strength to stay creatively centered, steady, fully receptive, fully giving, spontaneous, and actively accurate without procrastination.

Great actors/actresses and other great artists know this and know how to do it in portraiture, big or little role.

Great lovers know this and do it.

Great persons know this and do it.

Overall, there are very few truly great actors/actresses, artists, lovers, and persons in this world of ours.

Why? Perhaps it's because those few don't take themselves seriously, only their work and relationships.

Self-serious and play are antonyms. No playful kid is self-serious but....

Self-serious reasoning rules the world
    &
That's how money got the crown, how the buck-fuck rules, why dominant males manipulate the tills,

and why all who require attention, help, and compassion are so often excluded: children, the poor, the homeless, the 'different', the mentally ill, the old, the prison population, non-whites, the nameless functionaries, the Native American, and animals.

Then, there's the issue of deep, male chauvinism. And earth.

All truly accomplished teachers know:

+ What to emphasize at any given moment.
+ Imaginative creativity is superior to 'analytical' creativity because the latter is dependent on the former.
+ If that's not honored, then learning becomes deficient and misshapen. It limps. Struggles.

Back to American nuts & bolts:

+ Performance actors, singers, and comedians are the most socially valued of all American Adult Kids.

And the better to the best to the greatest of them always give, give *personally:* give story, honesty, and self.

They carry our values, serve them to us, and wait to serve us again.

- We pay 'stars' well to be reliable companions who are somehow concrete *and* available—living examples of 'transcendence' of the mundane, the banal, the tedious, the inconvenient, the abstract, and the regular daily struggles. When they perform, they take us with them. We willingly go and surrender, surrender to the magic. They're the 'special beings' who never die even though their actual bodies go away. And they supply for us the opportunity for worship that obliterates abstractions and obituaries:

    They are the mortal immortals.

So, TMAA, The Modern American Actor/Actress, is:

Film/Television/Stage Actors
Athletes
Directors
Comedians
Agents/Managers
Cinematographers/Editors
Songwriters
Composers
Wrestlers
UFC/MMA
Screenwriters

Playwrights
Singers
Dancers
Designers
Models
Writers
Rappers
Fine Arts Artists
Musicians
Porn Actors/Actresses
Politicians/Lawyers/Clergy
Talk Show Hosts
Radio Hosts/Media Journalists/Reporters

Consider:

+ Every person in the world learns to act—to act is human.

Not to act is impossible.

To act is for the mind and spirit what water and air are for the body and living.

+ Imagination and fantasy explore the possible. The most basic expression of the possible and meanings is through *stories*—the ones we hear, read, see, and invent because

+ We cannot *think* deeply without stories.

We cannot *talk* deeply without stories
We cannot *live* deeply without stories.

They make us want to live *in* them....as memories, as fantasies, as a future, as intimacy, and for hope, strength, guidance, and courage.

- ✦ Actual presence of the good or destruction of the good is the only way to analyze and judge human actions because actual good is not relative unless distorted thinking and arbitrary reasoning makes it so.

As stated, living as human partially means distorted thinking that is rationalized, justified, and defended.

But the good does not conform to human thinking or reasoning. Quite the reverse. Humans either learn to recognize the truly good and how to think accurately or they eventually learn how the absence of the truly good empties them and they become a tiny souvenir of self in a side table with a few photos and scraps of paper, a paper clip, and a brittle rubber band.

- ✦ If the rich and wealthy do not learn to surrender to the truly good and engage in philanthropy and teaching, they buy their mental illness and coast in a bunker fog, impervious to the sun and preserving false forms of light.

Thoughts:

Why has America become the Happy Castle that it is? Because Americans overwork, over-worry, over-compete, and under-sleep.

Why do Americans do that? Because the pressure's on, the pressure to 'matter'—not be left out, rejected, excluded, 'ordinary'.

Yes, America is the mightiest workforce in the world and within that rampant urgency there's a *need for respite* from striving, uncertainty, and anxiety.

Respite in America is called fun.

Entertainment.

Good times.

Where else in the world is there a Disneyland, a Disney World, theme parks, amusement parks, carnivals, Race Tracks of all kinds, NASCAR, Las Vegas, So Many Sports, Hollywood, Monster Trucks, Award Ceremonies, Pro Wrestling, UFC-MMA, and so many toys and games, so much music, Harleys, role-playing, etc.?

Nowhere.

So....

The world symbolically loves that aspect of American culture and borrows deeply from America because America is accurately thought/felt/believed to be magical, successful, big, strong, and cool—the location of The Happy Castle.

A little deeper:

- ✦ A primary need is to *belong*.
- ✦ Another need is to *individuate,* even if that process paradoxically requires merging with the cultural collective—conforming. Americans conform a lot.

To counter conformism, Americans develop a personal role, costume it, and act it.

Ever see homeless persons, how he or she puts things and clothing together to make a statement of self *in spite of no money?* A little style....a symbolic costume or a mix of fashions and possessions so they *have a role* to play that makes them feel like they matter a little bit and, therefore, are somehow recognizable and *seen*.

So....

If you and your role are an authentic match, you'll become engaged in the 'art' of living who you truly are: creatively productive of what's most actual for you to do because it's in your 'nature' to actualize. And you will know it as an evolving, wonderful self-portrait

Because....

For any person to be in the art of self and living means personal effort mirrors the integrity of greater and greater meanings through simplicity, clarity, diversity, enthusiasm, maturity, consistency, individuality, study, curiosity, discovery, and increasingly mature joy.

- We all have potential for greatness but few have potential for fame.

No famous person can experience fame when alone.
Any person can initiate great meanings anytime.

Through actions of greatness, we directly or vicariously experience time freed from our pressures, worries, fears, abuses of time, and our anxieties. That's how hope is answered.

So....

- A *great* person always reveals *beauty* as the symmetry of love.

Ultimately, that's what the best talent in any field does. A great actor or actress, artist, teacher, parent, researcher, physicians, nurses, engineers, workers, and so many others in all areas of endeavor do just that—they infuse time with beauty, the beauty of natural symmetry. And we recognize it so easily. That's why we're *moved* and why they're great at what they do, and why we're so grateful, respectful, appreciative, and dependent on the greatness of the few for our fuel.

Related to that:

The beauties humans make mark the universe.
When I say 'mark the universe' I mean it.
We can do that. And we do it.
I can't explain it but I know it. Not as belief but as true fact.
It happens every day.

Side note:

I remember the first time I *heard* classical music. Tchaikovsky's Piano Concerto #1....

Territorial Hall, a dorm. University of Minnesota.
October, Freshman year. Just out of Wyoming.
Biggest building I'd ever been in. Got lost after a shower. Had to go to the front desk where students and parents mingled, and stand there, waiting with a towel around my waist....asked for my room number. The girl smiled....and finally said 'Room 366....James'.
Later....
Standing at my dresser near the door....I placed the armature on the spinning 33rpm record and waited. The music began. I nearly fainted.
Next was Rachmaninoff's Rhapsody On A Theme Of Paganini. Suggested by a girl in Italian class. Toni.

Since then, the only thing I've ever binged on is beauty and thinking....been half way round the world, in all the heres and theres, seeking, noticing everything, absorbing nature, and marveling at the intimacies of human creations, the sanctity of nature and animals, and the beauties of the human body.

Struggle, perseverance, delight, desire, and curiosity have made me who I am. And I'm really slow so I've lived in huh a lot—puzzled, mouth hanging open, and eyes wide with wonder most of my life. But I'm lucky because I've lived as though pushed from the back and pulled from the front toward everything I didn't know was me. And I was unable to stop, even though I was looking around and saying 'Yeah, but what about this and that, and this and that and that over there and I'd like to do that....huh?'

So I'm writing this book about this and that, this way and that way, which means I can't separate living from divinity and divinity from beauty. And I can't articulate what I see, hear, touch, and live. That's deeply frustrating but not discouraging.

I'm a child with a very small vocabulary about all of this, and that will never change, even if I knew all the words in the world.

Side thought: what a cool person actually is....

In daily living, beauty is observable in persons who are really in touch and know how to express that in-touchness through their presence (simple cool), their action accuracy (actuality cool), and their goodness (spiritual cool).

We're attracted to those persons.
They're meaningful folks.
And we know it.
They have truth.
We want it.

They inspire.
They give.
They help make breathing worthwhile.

Pretenders in any area of effort can't do that.
There are many pretenders.

Consider....

As you know, being an actor in America isn't considered mature because it represents, like most careers in the arts in America, the absence of the practical and, therefore, a kind of weakness that points to not having fully 'grown up'.

What is *growing up*, anyway?

Emphasize 'up' in a non-spatial way and *up* then means growing *into* truly positive meanings by becoming more responsible and more completely able to integrate actual facts, time, effort and a solid set of values that secure love by coordinating thinking, living, and loving....and, therefore, experiencing enough happiness and fulfillment till you die. All of that's implied by the word 'mature'.

So...

My advice:

Become you. It's not easy, not a yellow brick road.... it's a wilderness you were made for. Look for it, be patient, let it find you, be willing to change, and enter it. Do it. Then let it take you all the way from in to deep win, within love.

Definition: drama....what *is* drama?

Well....it's the intensification of human experience....
And it's basically either artistic or non-artistic.

Non-artistic drama occurs spontaneously in nature, in our environments, and internally: it happens, it happens in us and it happens *to* us.

Artistic drama is designed: we make it.

There's a *third* kind of drama I'll mention later.

Consider:

Everyone thrives because of *drama* and for drama.

Simply stated, living is drama & drama is living.

And, as stated, play is one profound aspect of personal drama because it's *intrinsic,* part of the miraculous effort to develop from a what to a genuine who—'doing' that is expressive of one's 'I' becoming the 'me' of self….that developmental progress representing the inseparable why-how of all we do naturally: talk, think, imagine and explore, decide, research, share events and feelings and hopes and dreams and pain and bodies, losses, opinions, food, thoughts, attitudes, jokes, problems, struggles, pleasures, desire, fantasy, and fear….

That means:

We're always trying to figure something out.

We're always trying to figure someone out.

We're always trying to figure self out.

We're always trying to find a way 'in' or 'out' so we can be 'into' something that helps complete our 'me'

&

We're always looking for ways to stori-fy our experiences and make 'em count, make 'em matter, and enjoy 'em so we can *sense how we matter* through what we do.

We're wired for drama.

We dig it.

Drama to *melodrama*....

In America, the most popular form of drama is melodrama.

What is it?

Melodrama basically is truncated, highly edited drama juxtaposing good and evil without depth.

And the good wins.

American Entertainment basically *is* melodrama.

We love it and rely on it so we can somehow enjoy and re-enjoy values, beliefs, safety, thrills, reassurance, and some wows.

From that, a few entertainment nuts & bolts facts:

- American entertainment is commerce and an addiction.

That means....

- Americans aren't often fascinated by the deeply actual.

That means....

- American entertainment helps Americans to be positioned beyond danger, disturbance, intrusion, inconvenience, change, and *anxiety*.

That means....

+ American spiritual security subtly relies on entertainment.

That means....

+ American Entertainment is the primary guardian of the American good.

That means....

+ American entertainment is the collective American Community Hall, 24/7.

Imagine removing all media and social media from America for two months. No music, no television, no film, no entertainment, no games. Nada. Anywhere. Just the actuals of daily living.

The nation would convulse and collapse.

That's why....

Americans pay for The Modern American Actor no matter what it costs, pays to see them for a continuous supply of....melodrama as: laughter, action, violence, romance, gossip, guidance, intrigue, reinforcement, cool, winning, horror, perversion, medical safety, police integrity, evil, good, sentimentalism, challenge, beauty, justice, victory, identity, values, fashion, style,

principles, respite, voyeurism, sex, mystery, danger, supernatural, revenge, suspense, thrills, and meanings
&

The Modern American Actor willingly gambles on working again....waits, works, gets paid again, gambles, waits, works maybe, and gets paid again, maybe....for as long as the wheel turns favorably

Because

They know the Entertainment Wheel never stops, and just as it raised them to favor and tenancy it also lowers them to irrelevance and eviction.

Some sooner than others.

Flipside facts:

- ✦ Because TMAA wants to work, needs to be appreciated, tended to, wanted, and favored, TMAA pays attention to *business*.

- ✦ Most actors/actresses with over twenty years in the saddle have nurtured a work-niche that's somewhat set. But continuing to work is not guaranteed for anyone, *ever*. So, once audiences like you, label you, and aren't burned out on your 'brand', they place you more solidly in a category and you stay there for those who cast you, buy you, and pay for you. You try to maintain favor by not noticeably changing you or how you do your work.

Nuts & Bolts

Side thoughts:

Once the actor finishes some form of preparatory study and/or is working, he or she tends to lose motivation to study directly because it's time to *get work* and keep it coming—seek opportunities to get ahead, advance, be known, and have good representation.

This approach is partly due to the way Americans tend to think about education—as a tool for getting started on a winner's journey. That's valid up to a point.

On the other hand,

All deeply motivated persons in the medical field, the sciences, technology, sports, and physics etc., know that continued study and training are essential. But the actor/actress finishes studying/training, calls it a day, then begins the quest for work, and maybe takes workshops or classes here and there, consults a coach occasionally, and keeps rollin'.

Side question:

What's the difference between studying and training?
    Basically....

The former is informational. It leads to appreciative awareness and a retention of facts to be talked and/or written in varying ways.

The latter is experiential. It leads to cohesive doing in a particular area of study; it results in the integration of information and skills and increased capability for refined effort.

Basic studying leads to creative control. Stasis.
Basic training leads to guided play. Progress.

Control appeals because it's 'safer'.
Creative play is exciting. Safety's not a factor.

Training eventually absorbs studying and control through learning to guide play freely and accurately.

Complete acting culminates creatively in portrayal rather than a crafted performance. The cognitive and imaginative merge, which enhances intuitive awareness and release of effort rather than the execution of calculated, formulated, and planned acting.

So....

The guiding experience of creative play in acting is *intimacy,* personal involvement with what is guided: thoughts, feelings, imagination, purpose, language, and conclusions in the receivers—other players and the audience

Because....

The audience needs to understand your information so they can understand you, what you mean, who you are, and what you're trying to get done. They need to 'join up' with you rather than watch you. To do this well, you must be believable—acting must be personal before in can be interpersonal, and it must be interpersonal or it's isolated and not believable.

So:

To be increasingly believable requires sensitivity to words and humans, full dependency on receivers (cast and audience), and learning how the tensions of *living* (the drama) extend *into* the make-believe as motions of emotion: language and movement in human relationships—to self and others.

That means:

Feeling is interior, personal.

Emotion is conative—the purposeful release of feelings from the personal to the interpersonal: effort must be *aimed*. Genuinely.

And that means:

Words, gestures, silence, and stillness must attempt to penetrate the receiver.

Penetrate—go *into* the humanness of the other person and evoke reactions that become responses that can be followed sensitively, empathically, and curiously.

So....

'Being' is the first priority.

'Doing' is the second priority....because doing depends on being, just like living.

However....

Both require 'technique' and 'artistry'—the intuitive guidance of increasingly mastered skills....unified by deep respect for the complexity of experience implied beyond words *and* by the desire to live fully into 'look who I get to be and look what I get to do'.

This dynamic wholeness of effort is the essence of superior in contrast to inferior play: portraiture vs. performance.

Technique and artistry require training over and over, and study over and over until fully humanized acting occurs confidently in contrast to imitative acting.

Very basically, primary acting skills are:

- Learning how to *read words experientially*.
- Learning how to *see structures of language*.
- Learning how to *relate with others genuinely*.
- Learning how to *stay centered humbly*.
- Learning how to *think for the possible*.

Fact nuts:

+ Reading for acting is different than text analysis or dramatic analysis.
+ If schools and teachers do not make that distinction early, clearly, and accurately in ways that facilitate the ease of purposeful make-believe, then less valid instruction will occur.
+ If the Basic Skills are not established from the beginning, then moving on into additional areas of training/study wastes time, money, and students.

Bolts directly related to that last statement:

+ For acting students, there's a traditional glossary of terms generationally forwarded.
+ The Glossary indicates what acting entails, but glossary words are abstractions often used by teachers as the basis for teaching acting by *explaining* acting and giving notes.
+ If acting is explanatory before it's experiential, the result tends to be 'thought'-oriented acting: directly applied analysis of objectives, actions, super-objectives, backstory, character, inner monologue, arcs, spines, and beats, etc.

Performance is assembled, *crafted:* calculated and acted. The experience of *portraiture* does not occur.

So….

Premature use of The Glossary ends up to be inhibitory rather than liberating.

Why?

Well, glossary words easily can become 'things' to hold on to when more complete creativity isn't happening

    &

imagination is demoted in favor of thinking and explaining

    &

acting then becomes seriously sincere instead of playfully sincere…it becomes an adversarial task, a challenge the student/professional must face and defeat—conquer in order to win and not 'lose', lose being 'good', lose career stability, lose favor, and be faced with The Great American Antonym: ordinariness.

That said:

There is no exact step-by-step process to learning about acting. There is a structure, however, that moves from the introductory to the refined. Teaching, therefore, must be flexible and highly creative through emphases that are introductory to 'being' for the enhancement of 'doing' derived from one inescapable fact: *imagination is superior to analysis.*

Only through high receptivity to suggestion/impression can any reliable impulse/analysis occur, and that should feel like insight rather than logic, more like play than struggle.

So:

To make analysis reliable requires activating what *precedes* it—emphasis on how to read to receive impressions and perceive structures, and how to unite all impressions and insights toward the *task of self-talk* so complete 'living acting' can occur rather than crafted acting.

Developing this 'self-talk' is a highly personal aspect of exploring how to arouse self toward an increasingly complete union with script/role/others—the readiness to play openly, freely, and inquisitively in relationship as a different kind of self: that means entering the script, opening self to script and others, and learning how to bring forth a portrait.

Directors, writers, actors/actresses, and teachers who are sensitive to these facts know what I'm writing.

All of this obviously reveals:

I'm an adamant proponent of appropriate, continuous study and training for the refinement of effort and effect.

That means I also believe:

Artistic growth must be complemented by personal growth. The two go hand in hand because aging into roles of greater complexity requires increased sensitivity and flexibility to and for the demands and subtleties of language and living. Lack of maturity automatically prevents fuller artistry—*nuance* related to *poise:* learning how to nurture valid insights to address the ever-shifting balance of *being while doing*....to produce utmost personal engagement with language, the shifting moment, and full communicative clarity in relationship.

Nuance and poise are not often considered thoroughly or mentioned regularly by those who discuss American acting.

However....

Consider:

- Americans' love of melodrama precludes the necessity for fullest nuance and pcise in modern American acting.
- Melodrama often squeezes the talented actor/actress into tiny spaces for acting....like working out in a 4 × 4 × 5 foot room and pretending it's a gym. Acting is skillfully reduced from living fully to behaving intensely in ways that satisfy the minimal demands of what is required by producers, directors, writers, and the audience.

Nevertheless....

Even though options for work may or may not be numerous, the quality of the writing often ho-hum, and the constraints of the work environment limiting, the actor/actress knows he or she will be obsolete one day; so do the best work possible, adapt to working conditions, and just keep on going because.... American Society, as stated, is governed by the rise of a new generation who want *their own pantheon* and The New, the fresh. Not the old. No one wants the old for much of anything.

The Happy Castle

The old has to *feel new* because otherwise old old is old, and old is just that—not new, not exciting. That's partly valid but it's also an American cultural failing.

That means....

The wheel turns and older to old folks/actors everywhere lose relevance except during Presidential elections.
&
Only a few in show biz retain varying degrees of respect from peers before everyone in their age bracket dies.

For younger folks, most of the names on the sidewalk near Grauman's Chinese Theatre in Hollywood are just names in pink stars....that get walked on all the time.

I was talking to a kid here at the cabin a few days ago after he'd dug holes in hard soil for trees. He'd never heard of Marlon Brando. Pacino. Maybe Halle Berry. He wasn't sure.

Related to being a fan....

Every actor/actress tends to feel some measure of awe when in the presence of a great or more prominent or more influential actor, or a legendary 'star'.

Awe is part of mini-divinity actor-magic. And it's irresistible unless you're determined to be aloof and not get sucked in, which means you're insecure and already sucked in but you just can't admit it openly. Privately, however, you feel what any fan feels—wondrousness, maybe some envy, and the thrill of Raw Fan Amazement.

That also means....

There's a mesmerizing quality when seeing a brilliant actor/actress working or, in many cases, just seeing a famous person who represents and symbolizes part of your longing.

So....

If you've ever been out socially and someone says 'Look, there's so and so (a star)', can you avoid looking? Not really.

Why?

Because mini-divinity in the flesh is the concrete presence of an object of worship. And Americans have a profound need for concreteness and for worship. That's increasingly due to the breakdown of conventional-traditional worship structures and belief systems that don't work as fully as they could.

From those statements I mean....

Abstract 'faith' is less influential today
    &
entertainment provides a bridge
    &
TMAA is on the other side of the bridge.
And Americans go to them as the focal points of secular holiness.

The bridge is The Lens.

That means:

TMAA has become the dominant way Americans can participate conveniently in the crossover from daily living to something magical, e.g., spiritually engaging—intimately away from the actuals, the pressures, the worries, the lies, the striving.

However, when there's a crisis no one prays to TMAA. Most folks take the traditional Big Leap Approach and earnestly surrender in fearful or grievous need and longing for care and safety, and for healing and guidance associated with the God in Judaism and in the American Versions of Christianity. Even then, however, words of TMAA can and do give support to prayers and a lift to the spirits of those in crisis.

To reiterate….

+ To act or not to act?

That you will 'act' is a given.

+ Your choice of direction for acting will have a social name, a label; it will name you as a kind of person, the 'who' you will 'become'.

If what you've chosen is a 'false' you, your journey from matter to mattering will be a false ride. Disappointing. And you might sense it, adapt, and adjust but….or maybe you'll reach out in your middle years and take some rides….find your 'self' more completely by developing the strength, courage, and willingness to become who you most truly are by doing it, doing you; you'll discover the role you act will not be an act, but you will act it authentically.

For the actor/actress, that's sort of a paradox because 'self' is organized around opportunities to be other than self, self waiting to participate in being a different kind of self so the actor/actress can feel like a self.

Side note:

Wyoming. Sunny day, Akita asleep, Dodge diesel in the garage, snow melting, jeans and snap-shirts ironed, and trees waiting for late April so they can grow, get closer to being tall enough to put some shade on this 650 square foot old cabin.

Jack once asked:

'What are you doing here? What's *your* role? Who are *you*?'

I looked at him.

He nodded. Said he'd write me a note one day.

Mild summary:

So far, the basic nuts and bolts of America & Acting have been introduced. The rest of this book will address how to put nuts and bolts together and tighten 'em down a little for further consideration.

So....

How Modern American Acting Began

About sixty-five years ago, a group of folks unknowingly completed the last stand against the British. When they were done, another aspect of the American Revolution was over. Marlon Brando delivered the message
&
The rise of The Modern American Actor began.

Openly or quietly, British actors and actresses slowly acknowledged Brando's message and what was going on. They had to.

American actors and actresses began to Americanize acting more deeply to fit the American Way, the way of the personal in contrast to form, aesthetics, and tradition. Language had to flow *through the actor* before it came out of the mouth.

Acting couldn't be like acting.
And it couldn't be like living.
It had to *be* living....
So....

Types of actors and actresses began to emerge more completely, and with that development came the individual styles of acting we've come to know so well.

That meant....

Montgomery Clift, Spencer Tracy, James Cagney, Kirk Douglas, Barbara Stanwyck, Edward G. Robinson, Humphrey Bogart, Katherine Hepburn, John Garfield, Broderick Crawford, Burt Lancaster, Joan Crawford, Ernest Borgnine, Robert Mitchum, Gregory Peck, Karl Malden, John Wayne, Gary Cooper and others were slowly replaced by...

The New Actors:

Marlon Brando, James Dean, John Cassavetes, Joanne Woodward, Anthony Quinn, Geraldine Page, Paul Newman, Lee Marvin, Eva Marie Saint, George C. Scott, Rod Steiger, James Earl Jones, Patricia Neal, Jason Robards, Kim Hunter, Eli Wallach, Shirley Knight, Ruby Dee, Maureen Stapleton, Sidney Poitier, Ben Gazzara, Kim Stanley, the unsung presence of Gena Rowlands....and all other role-carriers of new acting called The Method....

How Modern American Acting Began

And they:

….were closely followed by Steve McQueen, Robert De Niro, Morgan Freeman, Anne Bancroft, Diana Sands, Al Pacino, Ellen Burstyn, Gene Hackman, Dustin Hoffman, Harvey Keitel, Tommy Lee Jones, Diane Keaton, Jack Nicholson, Annette Bening, Denzel Washington, Susan Sarandon, Sean Penn, Alfre Woodard, Jeff Bridges, Glenn Close, Angela Bassett, Jessica Lange, Laurence Fishburne, Ellen Barkin, Sigourney Weaver, Frances McDormand, Viola Davis, Tom Hanks, Forest Whitaker, Brad Pitt, Tom Cruise and scores of other gifted actors/actresses here and abroad—all influenced by the ineradicable presence of Brando….the OG Bad Boy, laden with enough charm, charisma, poetic aloofness, and talent to mesmerize audiences and inspire the young to define their work through *American potency:* toughness, resiliency, arrogant cool, quiet disregard, vulnerable isolation, defiance, and more honest acting centered in the human experience that also *included* a script.

Today's leading actors/actresses almost unanimously, one way or another, honor Brando. Why?

He basically defined American acting and influenced further release of the modern American Actress as a powerful presence heard in Man Clubs across the nation, heard and slowly acknowledged. Part of that evolving, multiracial, multiethnic power march has been enhanced by the repetitive artistic clarity of Meryl Streep.

She cannot be denied.

So, Brando's legacy:

Be authentic, 'cool', and unrelenting….and be *present*.

And do all of that at the *pace of living*.

To a degree that pace has been altered: the speed of American acting today tends to be slow or quick…. dramatically self-indulgent in varying ways and/or superficially dramatic and intense—not fully balanced within the complex flow and scope of human interactions as they actually happen. When this occurs, the wholeness of humanness is reduced to the immediately dramatic, and acting unintentionally becomes melodramatic: intense involvement with feelings, behavioral characterizations, attitude, and force.

All that said….

Ultimately, Brando shifted American acting from stage to screen. And there it remains, with localized, residual respect for theatre work.

So:

Modern American Acting now is defined by *film acting* as a symbolic zenith of acting.

Hollywood-America attracts the world's greatest talents. But....

Brando still keeps the penthouse in The Happy Castle.

Like no other known actor in the world, he remains an original in whom 'artistry and meaning' intersected briefly and deeply; and for a moment, his light illuminated existential mortality as ordinariness, anonymity, exclusion, pain, and longing....
&
The American male, through him, found a more vital way to feel American manly—strong, cool.

But...

That manliness was shaken by the Vietnam incident. Why? Well, America was losing its military virginity, suffering its first narcissistic blow....defeat. That shook things up; America's manliness got wobbly. Went to its knees. Held on to the ropes.

Then....along came Sylvester Stallone with *Rocky* and *Rambo*. In the evolving legacy and profound cultural importance of comic book heroes, imbued with indomitable spirit and a ruthless desire to win for the good, males once again found something more than ropes to hold on to. Stallone's lead males helped restore and concretize American 'manhood'. Part of that success is due to the influence of....

Mr. Brando,

Who stood alone and knew others would try to join him.
    They tried then.
    They try today, males and females.
    Benignly, he knew he had no company.
    And it didn't matter.
    That's one aspect of the irony of his greatness.

His work and person continue to influence how directors, producers, agents, and managers automatically assess actors and actresses.

He was Drama-drama but never quite melodrama.

His best work was 'beautiful' because it was a mix of the poetic, the spontaneous, the religious, and an unarticulated longing filled with mute desire held in eyes that spoke through a very thin veil: he was of the 'earth'—filled with that compelling mix of male and female, the crude and refined embodied within an unexpressed, vulnerable 'spirit' suggesting the 'divine' of humanity trapped in all of us by tradition, indoctrination, rules, and flesh.

His throne remains vacant, his domain untouched but gone.

That's a lot of praise for one actor. Rightly so. Original talents deserve such honest adulation, admiration, and respect because 'originals' in all areas of human endeavor are extremely rare.

Could he have learned more? Been better? Sure. That's generally true for every actor and actress. But he was troubled and got lazy, disenchanted. And older.

Nevertheless....

Mr. Brando unintentionally set the standard for the basic integrity of acting artistry. And because of that, American Acting got *better*.

It will continue to get even better as long as aspiring actors/actresses who are deeply talented and equally hungry reach for the stars unpretentiously and wisely, aloof from the seductive aspects of fame, justifications for laziness, and protracted plateauing—anything that impedes the continuity of educating their talent further toward, perhaps, genuine *mastery*.

What is Modern American Acting today? Easy question, complex answer.

The short answer:

First, theatre has gone the way of letter writing and conversation. Americans increasingly embrace The Lens as The New Theatre and The New Way to Read and Learn.

Second, Film, Television, and the Internet are revising acting by reducing language and humans to fit story patterns that please audiences who prefer to have designed emotional and physical contexts surround them and translocate them.

There are numerous other fantasy resources available. All of them represent the basis for the diversity of American Entertainment contexts. Lotsa choices. That fact is obvious. What's not so obvious is the commerce of entertainment. It's complex, aggressive, and risky because America is primarily about *business* and winning. Period.

That means....

Only the artist can afford to care about his/her art.

Beyond that, it's commerce and politics.

Right beside those facts....

Screenwriters usually write parts—not roles—governed by how a movie/film/series has to be written to get financing and distribution. Even 'renegade' series are designed cleverly with fresh surprises and 'new angles'. But the designs are familiar and, in the end, intact as parts: types with matching appearance, behavior, attitude, dialogue, and morality. In the end, it's melodrama. Variations on a theme of sameness.

That means....

American Acting today is absorbing TMAA and reshaping what they do and how they must do it.

That said, there's still a lotta good acting going on. Always will be.

A few more facts:

- Theatre's no longer influential except as the most concentrated, basic exposure to the dynamics of acting, writing, producing, and viewing. Therefore, rigorous acting programs are very important but each is only as good as its teachers.

- Theatre's no longer much of a resource for casting or showcasing fresh playwrights and young actors/actresses. And it doesn't attract seasoned actors/actresses often. Why?

It's expensive, risky, and usually not profitable. It can't be easily seen by many, no matter how long it runs. Theatre has succumbed more completely, like education, to commerce. But it will survive.

- As stated, business wins. Art loses. That's the American Way because the arts have never been truly important to Americans. We don't have the cultural longevity and maturity for such a wonderfully indigenous presence to occur.

In short,
American culture is a raft on the ocean….with two very strong oars named The Good and The Money. Overall, Americans don't know how to coordinate the oars very well for better rowing. That's the why of the American Predicament.

Cosmic & global facts:

- Earth is an anonymous planet in all of space.
- Living on earth depends on the duration of the sun and on the decisions of mankind.
- Eventually, the sun will go out; earth will perish.
- Humankind is in Chronic Self-collision.
- Religion is increasingly peripheral, existence is increasingly impersonal, and technology is increasing its presence in daily living. All of these variables contribute to rising anxiety and irrational, arbitrary reasoning.
- Globally, humans are fearful of the *new*, its risks, and challenges.
- 'Nature' is being replaced; we are leaving 'nature', leaving it to photographs, sightseeing, flowerbeds,

landscaping, zoos, commercials, woodsy walks, woodsy/wild reality shows, aquariums, and The Weather Channel.

- The replacement of nature will alter our nature because we will have altered nature. That's tragic.
- We're choosing the reasoning of the technical and personal reasoning over reason. The *telos* of love is wandering.

All of this suggests and reveals the growing presence of....

- *Autopia* in contrast to *utopia*....
- Autopia is retreat into the personal, away from the traditional-communal and the traditional-collective—into the world of self and The Lens.
- Autopia is, through The Lens, providing new versions of socializing, communing, thinking, and creating.

As you already know, there's an irreversible drift into altered forms of intimacy that include more personal control, less interpersonal involvement, less conversation, discussion, vision, thinking, and art.

That's the downside, maybe, but the upside has to be seen as part of the proliferation of cultural creativity that's the hallmark of American business, commerce, and entrepreneurialism centered on the possible.

Related to that....

The longing to belong and worship remain undiminished. That will never change. But how one finds belongingness and worship in America *is* changing; it's changing away from the deeply familiar toward the new: a startling head-butt with true facts is occurring. Youth gets it but older to old folks tend to resist with whatever influence is theirs to wield.

That means a lotta turmoil going on and a lot more to come.

That said....

Autopia will always include TMAA, and Entertainment will continue to be the nation's omnipresent, most reliable companion.

Pets will always be available, the word God among them.

But....

If the courage to ask questions and develop answers leading to action continues to wane and we are no longer able to see stars breathe because our attachment to detachment is winning, we'll submit.

We'll accept doom as part of the human situation....
&
We'll cope with the primitive terror that started our journey toward what we are today. And there, in terror, held and caged in a free fall without motion, the fact of dying will grip us with increasing pressure. The only sensation of 'life' will be the gnawing of spiritual termites eating thought after thought and meaning after meaning until all collapses, condemned, and, eventually, removed by time.

We'll know we are *so* tiny and *we did nothing to mark the universe* with love because the divine in us was almost eliminated or disregarded and denied before we distanced from it into our stylized separations of....

Autopia.

Flipside....

✦ Many folks will continue to create the good so the rest of us can continue to struggle, cross our deserts beneath stars, and somehow still find truth against the wars we have made.

Those folks will do what they do for us and for the cosmic dreams that need us.

If we develop more courage to see those dreams, see their designs, their significances….and respond by playing for them, playing thoroughly and for keeps, they will guide us.

- Great actors and great directors and writers and artists and designers and great editors and cinematographers and great composers and teachers and musicians and physicians and engineers and nurses and mommies and daddies and families and clergy and leaders and friends, children, and everyone in living pursuit of true 'stars' are the ones among us who will always remind us of what ultimately ensures survival—beauty, love, justice, power, life, truth, spirit, flesh, food, laughter, guts, and never say die until it's time for that. Then keep going.

The war of stars….is actual. And all wars must be measured, assessed, and evaluated by preservations of love.

So….

Bottom line, we are:

Justice
Sex
Hope

How Modern American Acting Began

Biz
God
Right
Wrong
Good
Evil
Religion
Defeat
Pleasure
Survive
Lust
Hope
Babies
Abstinent
Nature
Caress
Alone
Fear
Rape
Anxiety
Worship
Pain
Silly
Violation
Suffering
Struggle

Courage
Abuse
Vain
Victory
Search
Loss
Trust
Waste
Smile
Make
Cope
Murder
Neurotic
Ignorant
Reach
Retreat
Longing
Endeavor
Waver
Diversity
Unity
Play
Risk
Love
Humankind
Kind human
    &

all other words that honestly and accurately characterize the grisly and the grand of our species.

All that said, back to....

Modern American Acting....it began at a time when this nation was in a very significant shift.

So much has happened since 1950....

- Part of it's a runaway truck.
- Part of it's a profound beauty opened by those who research and invent for the good of people, animals, and the planet.
- Part of it's the wildflower magic of the Internet, social media, movies, films, music, singing, dance, and instant communication.
- And part of it is living near an invisible, existential bomb that has no location.
- The state of the American Mind is no accident. It's a result. And it will continue to produce resonant insecurity, anxiety, avoidance, denial, discovery, beauty, courage, laughter, and shifts of emphases until disasters crack the American Trance and force us all to dispense with aspects of 'personal reality', arbitrary thinking, and denial by seeking more of what's actually true and needed. Personal opinions and cherished beliefs will be forced to deal with some

undeniable facts because the alternative will be to die sooner, tragically.

Yet, in spite of all the ups and downs....

TMAA's importance will continue to grow, not in stature but in Autopian saturation.

What erupted over sixty years ago through Brando & Allies now is in another transition....call it....

American Acting Today

What is it?

First of all, it's an activity.
Second, it has numerous styles.
Third, it's a pervasive presence.
Fourth, it's hugely symbolic.
Fifth, it stabilizes America.
Sixth, it's not confined to acting for pay.
Seventh, it's changing because of technology and The Lens.

All of that prominently includes….

THE LADIES:

Remove all females from performance media, what's left?
Just guys
Won't work.
Why not?

Again:

Take actresses away, what's left?

Take female singers away, what's left?

Take the dancers, the porners, the reality stars, and the models away, what's left?

Take female writers and other artists away, what's left?

Take female politicians away, what's left?

Take female entrepreneurs and scientists away, what's left?

Take female designers, nurses, physicians, what's left?

Take female teachers away, what's left?

Take great mommies away, what's left?—

Just guys.

So, it's clear that:

The female *is* essential.

That means irreplaceable.

But

Why is the female so deeply and truly needed in all American Performance Media and in daily living?

The cynic will have an answer.

However, for healthier and more honest folks, the basic answer is obvious—the female is super-special and carries a unique quality of actual divinity.

A little deeper:

What's not very often acknowledged is one fact: the solid, complete female—a woman—can *live* without the male or a partner.

Males don't understand how that's done because males can only cope and adapt, rationalize or lament, give up and go potato or cynic, catch another bus-ride relationship, or go lonesome.

What does this suggest? It suggests: without the female the male is functional but somewhat wayward, lost, and longing, and/or adapted to her absence in ways that numb waywardness, interest, lost-ness, and longing.

The female is not confined by flesh, gender, or dependency. For the male, it's different.

Females have babies, a way to nurture.
Males have ideas.
Both produce offspring.
One is conception.
The other is conceptual.

Creativity governs both efforts.
One usually is from the womb.
The other is from the brain.
Both cause excited anticipation of parturition.
Both are subject to stillbirth.

One is the object of love.
The other is the object of success.

One is not an experiment experience.
The other one is.
One is the flower of the universe.
The other is a garden hose.

That means:

The deepest blooms of the human experience are 'children' in any form.

Children, irrespective of age, are *meant* to develop, grow, flourish, enjoy, and know the good. They are flowers arching toward the sun. This is also true of the old and the bedridden, those in hospice, and the forgotten ones.

We're all children unless, as stated, we lose the willingness to play and nurture—bloom.

If we're not genuinely arching toward the sun *somehow*, what are we doing?

What's this got to do with America & acting?

A lot.

Any discussion of The American Actress requires noting the American Perception Of The Female in films, movies, television, all competitive media, society, daily living, the workplace, and homes.

That perception-perspective can only begin with the word 'marginalized' in contrast, obviously, to *centralized*—the most honest cultural and personal placement there is for her.

The female has been forced to thrive in the 'margins' of living, governed by the narrow range of options in every field of endeavor except childbirth. Then she's front and center because she's giving birth. But after that, she's often just a mommy—still marginalized and so often expected to remain primarily in mommy-land, and do it without being too bothersome, too vocal, too demanding, or culturally off-leash.

Typically, the American Male doesn't really think openly about the superior strength of the female and her potential to *change* American Culture for the *better*. That's too scary, so the male (in contrast to a man) tends to think about her sexually and on leash. A complete conformist.

The American Actress slowly is removing all leashes, all constraints.

The American Actress, as is the case for ladies in practically all fields, has truly begun to 'move in' from the margins to stay.

Fact….

If you look closely at the spirit that resides in the eyes of the solid female who has become a woman without imitating male ways, and if you're willing to see her and she's ready to *let* you see her, you will see what I'm saying is there—that superior strength—in spite of The History of The Leash.

It's in her eyes….unmistakably mirroring spirit all the way to soul.

Why does America need really good to great actresses? Well, because actors can't act what she alone can and must act: love; the dynamic presence of creation, potentially and actually. And from that presence, when the really good actresses do their best love-work, we see into their *power* as a sanctity because….

She….*is living womb*.

She….is creative *and* procreative in ways that make her meaningfulness undeniable, unless you're in denial.

She….is a glimpse of the unambiguous for which there are no words. And it is the unambiguous we all seek—no blurs.

Those glimpses occur
In song
In dance
In poetry

In prose
In any field
    &
In interactions with others.

Most of the time, however, in America and in the world, the glimpses occur anonymously through simple acts of love as kindness. That's not utopianism.

It's actualism of the deepest sort.

Which means:

Females seeking their fullest creative potential as women are driven by the need for dynamic, full actualism.

Great women of the world, whether anonymous or known, live within this drive.

Great actresses act within this drive.

So….

When the greatness of the female is reduced by isolating or leashing aspects of that greatness, then her strength, humor, and courage are edited into conformity without the depth of humanity so naturally and abundantly present in her. She's expected to fit into the culture and please the mental habits of aging males who don't really get what a woman is. For her, that's like wearing shoes that are way too small, all the time. For centuries.

Consider:

How The Public relies heavily on The Modern America Actor/Actress

    &

How The Public relies on melodramatic scripts that reinforce the dynamics of good and evil, right and wrong, justice and injustice, and the sacred

    &

How the relation of script to TMAA and to ethics/morals is a business imperative no sane producer will defy because they all know....

The Actor/Actress is already culturally pre-cast as:

- The good guy/girl, the bad guy/girl, and the in-betweens. 'Bad' guys are destructive of living.

'Bad' girls are destructive of morality.
Bad guys and bad girls must suffer and lose.
Good guys and good girls must struggle and win.
The in-betweens are support roles.

'Bad' guys destroy life.
'Bad' girls disregard purity.

Then there's comedy.
Comedy bypasses dramatic conflict in favor of dramatic tension....and no one loses.

Comedy lightens the moral code and load.

There's deep honesty and morality in great standup comedy.

Imagine removing laughter from living. Try that on for size. No laughter, ever. We couldn't do it. We'd make funny happen. Why is that?

What's laughter that makes it so holy?

What's the essence of an authentic smile?

Check out a great baby smile. Explain it completely. You can't.

The American Actress &....the sensual:

Sensuality is for humans what water is for flowers.
Sensuality is a *vital aspect of human nature*.

However....

The cultural evolution of Moral America has included an increase in the decrease of sensuality.

The American answer to that decrease is to increase sensuality 'outside the rules'—rebel.

Consider:

+ When's the last time you were in church/temple/mosque and saw a beautiful painting or statue of a nude male or female, or heard exquisite poetry about the beautiful intimacies and longings of deeply experienced, appreciated, physical beauty and the mysteries of love?

- If beauty is suppressed or disregarded, living narrows, art narrows. This is easily observable in American society and in American artists.

Back on track:

The Modern American Actress has had a cultural assignment for decades—to be the primary source and answer to America's longing for beauty, the sensual, goodness, and for some of the 'rule-breaker/ball-breaker/heart-breaker' bad girl stuff. In America....

Bad sells.
Good secures.
Beauty enthralls.

Americans are always lured by the possibility of seeing breasts, abs, buttocks, and maybe....more. Producers and entertainment writers know this as part of putting most scripts together—if possible, got to have the peeks. It sells.

However....

The deeper need and fact in all of this discussion is the spiritual longing to see the *source* of creation on earth—the beauties of a woman's body and the goodness of her spirit.

The profoundly combined beauty/power of the female is one of two important actuality symbols on the planet:

She represents the continuity of life and the symmetry of love, *and* she brings the child; we are from she.

Facts reiterated:

- To *remove* sensuality from the spiritual is to ravage beauty.

- To *incarcerate* sensuality is oppressive, naïve, uptight, and narrowly self-righteous—destructive of beauty, destructive of truth, and destructive of wellness and well-being.

- To *honor* the human body respectfully, to dignify it—personally, medically, sexually, interpersonally, appropriately, openly, spiritually, and enthusiastically without ever cheapening its beauty in any way is so often lost in the pervasive wilderness of human reasoning and ways.

- Yes, The Modern American Actress is the primary recipient of American emphasis on the sensual and the beautiful. Sometimes, however, there are great roles that include her inimitable capacity to portray truths of love beyond appearance and the directly sensual.

Consider:

There's a huge interest in Red Carpet Action at the Academy Awards, SAG Awards, Emmy & Tony Awards, Beauty Pageants, Grammy Awards, BET Awards, etc.

No one shows up in dated jeans, flip flops and a bandana. But if an actress shows up wearing a dazzling string top, a designer thong, and heels....would anyone look? Sure, over and over.

Why?

Because, as stated, Americans need, really *need*, to see the sensual-sexy, the beautiful, the mysterious, the magical: the romantic glamour of the secular gods and goddesses....see 'em a little closer and listen to 'em being interviewed....it's all linked to the need to worship and adore something concrete, something magical and purely human....but somehow not.

So:

Gals wear gowns, jewels, hints, and reveals.

What can a guy wear?

There are only so many variations on a black suit, white shirt. And irrespective of what he wears, he's secondary to the ladies.

Guys aren't the focal point *at all*.

They never stand out, they stand around.

It's the ladies....and their glamour, their make-up, their faces and eyes and arms and 'the hiddens', the delights hinted at that we notice....and wonder about, wondrously.

It's normal to do that in a culture where the sensual has had to hide from Moral Robots.

Cynics and other discouraged lovers can easily get all bent out of shape, critical, catty, and sarcastic about glitz and glam. But comedians and the public who enjoy The Happy Castle and The Sun of Play also enjoy awards events because, if they're respected for their cultural importance, they can be fun, silly at times, and uplifting....another celebration of how humans try to mark the universe for 'stars' that do not war.

That means:

Awards ceremonies, obviously, were invented for participation in something *greater* than daily living—a fleeting translocation into the realm of something 'special'—*meanings*....just like the stories that take us out of this world, out of self, yet magically into self.

Back to The Actress:

How does she cope with the demand to serve America as part of the answer to America's Sensual Drought two centuries long?

She puts up with male chauvinism, paternalism, disrespect, condescension, bias, bigotry, racism, rejection, harassment, abuse, and other culturally pathological immaturities.

She looks for opportunities to *build* beyond the limiting premises of gender, appearance, race/ethnicity, and negative bias. She has to.

So....

America's leading and rising actresses continue to play the game to keep on working to win *legitimacy:* equal pay, respect, dignity, stature, significance beyond sensuality, and movement away from simple Content Scripts to Substance Scripts requiring deeply affirmative, personal *portrayals* of humanity.

Those opportunities are rare.

Age becomes a prominent factor.

It shouldn't.

Actresses positioned higher in the hierarchy of success seek work that integrates the harsh facts of Show Business & American Culture—they look for the best material available from Script World.

Or they produce their own projects.

This search/effort is different from that of...

THE GENTS:

Generally....

For guys, male beauty can be a barrier.

Rugged, ballsy cool, strong, and somehow interesting are the basic criteria for male leads.

Then there are the numerous types of 'character actors' and smaller support role categories.

As stated:

+ Brando's influence shaped the direction of acting for the American male and, therefore, for producers who continue to recognize how American male culture reflects a predisposition for competition, fighting, violence, winning, and 'cool'. So they generate most projects for American male actors to engage that way....as cowboys, boxers, vigilantes, rebels, lawyers, cops, soldiers, corporate entities, misfits, criminals, street guys, and superheroes.

American males don't like to feel weak.

American actors don't like to feel weak.

What does 'weak' mean for American males? The answers are well-known and well-traveled....and the beat goes on.

- Male roles primarily center around adversity and ways to win. It's an accepted mindset for actors, writers, producers, and directors.

That's why strong roles and 'strong' acting dominate American acting (including the ladies).

- Loosely, the actor-melodrama-man has been invented as one who's 'an individual', one who doesn't need anyone deeply, one who can tough it out under any circumstances, one who can get hurt, take beatings and wounds, and get back up again and again, and one who can do revenge for justice.

Melodramatic heroism.

And, as you know....

A play, screenplay, or script basically is a structure of actions in relationships from Point A to Point B.

The quality of that structure and writing determines the depth, fullness, and compelling-ness of story, dialogue, and relationships.

Writers consider what parts or roles are needed to make the writing work.

Writers know the protagonist has a problem or will be confronted by a problem that has to be solved.

Writers know everyone else plays a role helpfully, antagonistically, or functionally. In movies and television, this typically makes the tensions of conflict roll toward a resolution favoring the good and, perhaps, a sequel or a series if the project's a movie.

Good to brilliant structure and dialogue are fairly rare in all writing because *dialogue patterns* so often are part of *writing patterns* that serve *melodrama patterns* that are not the ways actual persons live, talk, and do.

And that directly shapes....

Melodrama & acting:

Specific melodramatic performance patterns have developed in the past thirty years....yet, the overall quality of acting is far superior to what it was.

Melodrama writing makes it easier to reduce depth.

To compensate for that reduction, actors/actresses tend to intensify feelings, behavior, and attitude to fit patterns centered on one or more themes: sex, romance, neurosis, noble suffering, betrayal, danger, confrontation, love, revenge, death, killing, and/or the need for justice.

These intense performance theme-engines easily become mood-modes of acting that are simplified, intensified, refined, repeated, stylized, and often imitated.

As a result, acting has been almost imperceptibly altered, causing a new norm that is also the basis for current evaluations, criticisms, and judgments of acting.

So:

Modern American Acting so often is more automatic—subtly slick—behaviorally and emotionally. However, the better actors/actresses always strive to authenticate emotionality and 'character'.

The New Acting Norm is, as suggested, largely focused on a strong performance derived from the union of feeling, stillness, directness, and an intensity of personal presence that dominates what has traditionally been called 'character'.

Few actors ever achieve full 'character' because it's not required; plus, it can be elusive due to unfamiliarity with what full character actually denotes and demands.

This means....

The New Acting Norm is shaping how so many actors/actresses self-stylize, costume, and perform a role rather than portray a person vulnerably and *comprehensively*.

&

American Acting Today

Broadly speaking, Acting is becoming more competitive—with self, the acting business, and time....
&
The New Acting Norm will continue to be altered by the demand for more special effects that will continue to reduce the depth of story and, consequently, the importance and richness of language. Increasingly, the actor will act among things and contrivances in a cast of altered humans and/or humanized animals.

Consider:

✦ Motion is *the* prominent aspect of American culture. The static is somewhat feared. Motion reassures.

Excessive need for motion—external and internal—is built into today's American World. And that need generally will increase because of the importance it has in reducing anxiety.

The most available source of 'motion' is The Lens. So....

✦ Technological motion through passive arousal is slowly replacing physical initiation of activity.

✦ The need for motion is partly why most plays don't appeal to most Americans. Not enough motion. Only talking. But musicals do move, and they're not 'serious' so they're okay. No one gets antsy.

+ The goal of nearly all producers is to secure a large audience by providing a product that's not troublesome, worrisome, or stupidly negative: find a way to score without alienating.

The products are 'containers' providing opportunities (trailers, teasers, marketing) for audiences to open them, look inside, and, hopefully, buy.

To reiterate:

+ America's intense need for stories and reassurance has caused the evolution of melodrama as *the* American domain of secular holiness with venue sanctuaries for the gods and goddesses.
+ Versions of American Entertainment permeate America to the extent that melodrama, politics, and religion in America are fused.
+ Melodrama is fully present in churches, congregations, homes, government, schools, American fiction, and in how we think, talk, and role-play behaviorally through clothing, fashion, 'style', attitude, and language. That's how influential and pervasive The Lens & melodrama are on the American Psyche.

In this sense, Americans are slowly turning all aspects of American culture into entertainment resources.

- America's attachment to entertainment, TMAA, and The Lens is a spiritual addiction because there is no alternative source for spiritual engagement: nowhere else to worship freely, concretely, communally, and on autopian terms.

So....

- Melodrama has become *the* American Cultural Companion. It's the basis for Brain Theatre and Self-casting, then taking a chosen role to clothing, language, demeanor, and to the public for display and confirmation.

- Thinking isn't real popular in America. Never was. Takes too much time. But role-playing and role-watching are popular....as part of America's reliance on....

Stories:

- *Stories* have become the ultimate American Safety Net, a net secured and re-secured daily through cellphones, social media, The Internet, and entertainment media—all available 24/7.

Stories are part of America's National Treasure Chest.

Stories are cultural cement, glue, and insurance. They guide thinking, reassure reasoning, and secure cultural pillar-visions of love, justice, hope, and the need for safety.

Stories are morality guides and mortality shields.

Stories that transcend content through 'substance' are called 'great' stories.

- *Stories* that are great are irresistible. They 'move' us beyond melodrama. They touch the edge of divine and intimate the validity of enduring the demands of enduring....all for love.

That said....

- TMAA is the key storyteller for restating America's noble highs—the greater meanings of living—and the ugly lows of lesser meanings....

....the beauty of One Side and the crassness of that Other Side where humankind is human-cruel, where there are no peaks, only the flats and darks, the stark alleys of 'evil' where destruction has no rules, where humans are targets of feelings, revenge, fists, words, and bullets, where children are less than pennies, where sex and love are cheapened, where there's a blind, tragic violation of body, mind, and spirit watched by audiences who delight in ruthlessness made available by profit-pimps who try to insert something redeeming amid the guns, revenge, bravado, sex, and rampant, unrestrained visual violence....

- ✦ Negative melodrama facilitates fantasy-devaluations of humans to objects for manipulation and destruction. This is usually done by male actors. But actresses recently have entered the arena to compete for the Crown of Kill.
- ✦ Many defend the violence as 'just movies'

But

Why do humans watch humans destroy other humans?

That's a question, not a criticism.

There's an answer.

A simple answer is: watching is a way of participating.

The kind of participation chosen reveals aspects of the viewer as a person.

- ✦ The collective dimension of Entertainment Watchers is called fans, watching what they *like* to see. Fans who share a similar attraction feel a bond and, if it's a big fan-base, the bond becomes cultural. But you know all this.

Consider:

If everyone on the planet learned to think, love, and live with improved mental health, increasing maturity, and generosity of concern for others, animals, and the planet, many of today's films, television programs, and other forms of entertainment would not be watched. The stories would not appeal.

ABOUT MASTERY
Consider:

- Mastery is an underrated, largely disregarded goal in living, loving, and work.

Sufficiency is more practical, less demanding. Easier.

However and obviously...

- Anything less than mastery in any area of living is an adaptation to mediocrity, levels of less....from matters of health and work to matters of thought, habits, love, money management, and faith.

And, lastly, art.

- Mastery in faith is an interesting topic rarely discussed for what it most actually is and most commonly isn't.

- The journey to mastery begins with the genuinely personal, authentic lure of the possible that, if answered accurately, always leads to discovery.... then, perhaps, to entry *into one's most valid affinity,* which slowly becomes a conscious effort to mature from crudeness to refinement through further education/training and continued study in whatever forms all of that can best occur.... and through *labor*—years of work to learn how to refine what is done for maximum, involvement, expression, and efficiency.
- Refinement of effort is the goal of technique.

Technique secures the potential for comprehensive integrity of expression through mastery of the basics in any area of endeavor.

Then, of course, there's *negative* creativity....and that's the basis for explaining the grisly struggle of human history and so much of current suffering.

- Mastery is not perfectionism. No human can achieve any aspect of ultimate perfection unless what's done is an act of genuine love—any act of kindness. Kindness requires no study or technique, only the inherent drive of the good to give and to receive.

- Mastery cannot be confined to or achieved by self-discipline, determination, or erroneously ascetic, calculated, behavioral devotion.
- Mastery is never clever.
- Mastery is the unification of valid aim and effort that eventually liberates the doer to participate fully in creativity in any field.

That fact represents the ultimate way of understanding the beauty of the word diversity, which means we all are unique and uniquely one, like all species—there's only one of each of us on this one planet, and there's all of us as one on the planet, along with all other species....some tragically diminishing due to our inability to value and dignify their uniqueness. So we kill them. Easily.

And we watch killing easily....unless it's actual, in front of us, without a Lens or a weapon.

Few persons encounter the animal spirit before killing it.

Because it's just an animal. Really?

Few persons actually experience raw, physical violence....the kind that cuts, breaks, bleeds, writhes, screams.

If lamb and veal are delights to eat, raise a lamb or a calf, then one morning take a very sharp knife, look the creature in the eyes, smile, then lift the chin of the calf or lamb, and slice deep. Watch the creature die.

The point is, when willful *destruction* of living or love is actually experienced or seen, it's a whole different ballgame.

Mastery related to acting:

There are few actors/actresses interested in full mastery because a successful career doesn't require full mastery.

That means:

Mastery in American Acting can be reduced to a very personal style that is defined by emotional honesty and intensity, and indisputable compelling-ness that causes popularity. There are numerous actors and actresses for whom this is true. And it often works for long careers.

About style:

Style, at its best, is not about personality. It's about the *way* you do your work….and the way *you* do the *work*. That means the evolution of 'self' slowly integrated into the work as an effort to refine the work by transferring

the *basics of acting* (living)
into
the *actions of acting* (doing)

so a script *lives* fully through *you* as it *lived* fully through a good writer, with all the appropriate nuances present in *living*.

That's not about personality; it's about personal artistry (playing completely and responsibly) in contrast to calculating (crafting), or competitively trying to prove you're 'good' so you don't get left out.

What are the basics of acting to be mastered so 'living acting' can be more complete?

Side note:

At one point, I received an MFA Degree in Directing.

A *Master* of Fine Arts Degree. I had no mastery.

I was a raw beginner with two years of exposure to basic info through tasks designed and aligned to function as classes that, when completed, would produce a Degree, which happened and....I remember thinking about that when I applied for a teaching position....I had a degree. Now what?

I've reflected repeatedly on that moment during the years of a long career. Mastery. Hmmm....

Thoughts....

- ✦ If excellent mediocrity is an acceptable standard, then further study/training is somewhat irrelevant and so is the topic of mastery until a master's effort moves you deeply to appreciative envy, and/or admiration and, perhaps, a personal comparison from which you discover aspects of your complacency and deficiency. Then you can either shrug, adjust and rationalize your passivity, or you can challenge yourself for greater learning and more complete work.

- No teachers challenged Mr. Brando's beautiful potential for mastery. So he mastered an aspect of artistry that became his style and, at times, coasted on that, used his name, tried to dismiss it all, and even tried to walk away from acting.

I believe he really knew what he let happen to his potential. Perhaps he was bored.

And who would have been the masters to teach him?

And what writers were writing the kind of language that would make him grow into his talent?

- It's very easy for anyone to spot an actor/actress whose artistry and mastery of the basics are fully present. They're so few in number they always stand out.

And it's easy to spot talented actors/actresses who have the potential for complete acting.

And it's easy to spot those who don't care about complete acting while they believe what they do *is* complete.

And it's easy to see those who do care but have nowhere to learn what's needed.

What are the criteria for excellence applied to TMAA?

They are but two: emotional honesty and intensity, and the word 'character'.

As stated:

- *Living* acting is a distinction Brando truly set in motion. That 'motion' is slowing and waning in favor of feelings, character, and a 'strong' performance.
- Portrayal is rare. This is partly due to writing that lacks mastery—substance in contrast to content—and the increasing presence and acceptance of melodrama and 'melo-acting'.

All answers to these assertions and questions are based on the *quality of ambition:* the ferocity of desire to do until reaching the limits of one's talent.

What I'm writing isn't irrelevant, but it is somewhat extraneous to American acting, so it seems irrelevant.

Side note:

On the wall above the desk where I'm seated, there's an old photograph of a cowboy, Bill Pawley, riding a saddle-bronc at a back-in-the-day, Cody, Wyoming rodeo.

I often look at the photo and take in the poise with which he rides and rhymes within the unpredictably familiar....no time for thinking, posing, or self-consciousness....just participate fully, take the risk, and do the challenge that potentially promises the possibility that the ride will be a deep thrill in the form of a great horse demanding all the artistry and technique a cowboy can bring—personal affinity, willingness, deep excitement, and whispers of appreciative humility added. It takes many, many rides to learn how to ride a bull or a bronc into a portrait....
    &

Any great rider knows he's not doing the ride, the ride does him....so he blends with it, into it, masterfully. He misses a beat, he gets bucked off. It's all in the millisecond details.

Back then a ride lasted till it was over or the rider was thrown. Today it's only eight seconds.

But this photograph isn't about time; it's about *timing*, and in this case the timing is a *portrait* of a portrait ride.

Great portrait photo, great portrait ride: life magically *lives*.

You have to have 'talented excitement' to ride broncs, bulls, love, and art.

Side note....

Lotsa movies have been made about cowboys. None capture true cowboy because 'cowboy' has become another premise for melodrama fantasy about what 'cowboy' is, looks like, talks like, and does.

True cowboys were and are few in number. The boots, hat, belt, spurs, chaps, saddle, horse, and bandana are living symbols within a unique personal world united with the natural world of air, animals, water, work, rest, eat, and do it all again because somehow it feels good and is good.

The cowboy codes of the Old West are mostly gone now. A true cowboy lived up to those codes as best he could, lived them into his art of living. That's how he put a life together while ridin' the prairie, doing his thing.

It was called 'makin' a hand'.

The best cowboys were master ropers, riders, trackers, and survivors. They read land and animals all the way to git 'er done. Every day. They had stamina, will, humor, determination, grit, and a greatness of heart that was honest, playful, and upright.

Mastery, for as long as it could last, that was the call.

And it extended to the ladies.

Then there were:
the pretend cowboys
the troubled ones
the ones who could've made it, maybe
and the wannabes who hung out in costumes and bars.

I see pretenders here in Wyoming.

I also see fellows whose hats talk years of hard weather and many chores, whose trucks talk labor, hay, dogs, goosenecks, trailers, more of that hard weather, many miles of highway and dirt roads, and cowboy gloves and boots talking stirrups, chaps, more hard weather, and many miles in the saddle.

From all of that comes honest cowboy faith....a way of worshipping what is found in nature and animals, and from listening close and easy on long rides to the lyrics of leather, weather, and solitude.

Today, it's all going away. Except for land. I'm glad I got in on it when I was a kid able to see and hear and

The Happy Castle

do it with folks who were part of the transition from the 1880s into the 20th century.

I absorbed and retained it....held on to it all stubbornly. I didn't know that because I never thought about it. My clothes, longings, and dreams were talking to me but I didn't put 2 and 2 together until thirty years ago when I started riding the dream adventure I'm doing right now.

I've taken the symbols with me for many decades. Had a chance at 21 to go full cowboy....that's another story. Wanted to but....I miss not doing that, miss it deep. I remember all the horses I rode, roping, rodeos....oh well....two roads diverged....

Back to acting and writing:

Screenplays used to be called Screen *Plays*.

Then the words were joined, with emphasis on the first syllable.

This permitted a separation from the play and the emergence of a new category of writing.

As you know,

Screenplays center on theme, concept, context, *circumstances,* and resolution.

Plays center on humans and a *situation* that may or may not be resolved.

A screenplay includes dialogue.

A play depends on dialogue.
Movies are mobile, 'activistic'.
Plays are stationary, linguistic.

Add all this up and you get:
Situation is more complex than circumstances.
So:
Complexity requires more talking.
Circumstances require more physical activity.

In screenplays, a problem is solved.
In plays, a problem is explored.
In screenplays, morality nearly always wins.
In plays, winning is of minor importance.
In movies, scenes are edited.
In plays, it's open the curtain and go till the play's over.
In movies, there's a score.
In plays, there is very little music.

In films, humans are symbols. Distantly present. *Real.*
In plays, humans are *actual*. Intimately present. Right in front of you, in costume and make-up.

Some films resemble plays. They're not as popular.
Some plays include audio/visual *enhancements*. That's about as far as a writer can go without altering the manner in which a play will be viewed.

Side thought:

In American education and daily living, there's a general disregard for words, yet there's always great delight in slang. We love slang because it's so experientially accurate and interesting. It lives when said. Just like purposeful swearing lives.

Basic delight in the use of language is, for TMAA, slowly being absorbed and replaced by silent language intimated with eyes, angles, editing, and the timing of movements that impart information the audience needs in order to understand what's going on in the actors/actresses and/or what's about to happen. And when there are words, they most often are, as stated, supportive: informational narrative for story continuity or emphasis, not language more deeply expressive of the complexities of living....so, mood, and emotional and physical context tend to dominate.

That means:

There's little time for the wholeness of experience to occur because experience is *framed* by acting that is *framed* by the moment that is *framed* in relationships *framed* by scripts from writers *framed* by The Business of Writing for movies.

So:

The only truly vital artistic venues where language still rules are in the work of great comedians and great rappers.

Nevertheless....

All of this discussion of basic acting, artistry, mastery, and language points to a time in every artist's life, when he or she was first smitten, became an aspirant, dreamed about, then decided to, as I once did....leap....

America & The Acting Student

—The America Part—

In two hundred and fifty years this nation, as you know, has become the mightiest military and economic power in the history of the world. That means all forms of napping in America have been eliminated except rest periods for wee ones in day care, for some preschoolers who aren't already fast-tracking, and for the old.

America has given the word 'laziness' a negative intensity akin to disease.

Why?—because of a cultural compulsion to win, somehow be acknowledged for 'getting ahead', 'making something of yourself', and making money.

Be special.
Stand out.

Related facts:

- Americans overwork and under-sleep. Americans don't stop.
- Reflection, meditation, contemplation, etc., are not part of most weekdays or weekends. Weekends are time for some fun, some entertainment, some 'go' time or 'do' time on personal terms. Or more work.
- America lives *very seriously,* almost fear-fully.... so....just keep going, make it happen, stay in motion, run the dream wheel....Slick Honey Blackjack Crown, puttin' it up and layin' it down....decade after decade.

That's productive but in obvious ways, very costly.

Ever see a disturbed person talking to imagined persons while standing obediently at an intersection and acknowledging a DON'T WALK red light figure? When the light changes to green, the person moves and takes the imagined world right along....in touch but out of touch with the fullness of what's actually going on: it's called being functionally disengaged: in a personal reality.

America & The Acting Student

That's an example of an extreme, dramatic Singular Trance in the generalized, collective experience called a Culture Trance. All countries have one.

- Cultural Trance isn't so obvious because culture is *collective conformity*. Everyone's basically doing the same thing in differing ways because of differing constraints on options due to differing incomes, classes, and liberties.
- Within America's Culture Trance are thousands of young persons driven to become part of the performing arts as singers, dancers, musicians, and students of acting.

Consider:

We can't really understand who we are personally unless we experience individuation through resistance to who we feel/think/believe we are.

We can't really understand who we are until we find a way to define—'see'—who we are. I think of this as the 'I of the eye and the eye of the I'. Both have to be a match to transcend the 'me' en route to a unified self.

If we're lucky and at liberty, we can recognize our greatest affinity, then go for it through education, stimuli, and encouragement. There's a lotta kids who don't get much of any of that.

But for everyone there are The Labels, and each of us becomes one of them or genuinely or imitatively.

They are the....

American Social Roles:

Biker
Corporate
Professional
Politician
Clergy
Cop
Physician
Sales
Educator
Mechanic
Plumber
Lawyer
Actor/Actress
Writer
Doctor
Dentist
Artist
Cowboy
Athlete
Rancher
Counselor
Therapist

Farmer
Assistant
Musician
Parent
Trucker
Server
Cashier
Host/Hostess
Receptionist
Care Giver
Spokesperson
Cook
Singer
Player
Office Worker
Laborer
Manager
Tech
Nurse
Criminal
Marginal
I Don't Know
Whatever
Homeless
Lost
Bouncing Around
Etc.

The list is longer.

American Social Roles have three images:

Cool
Not cool
Between cool and not cool

And

Many Stereotypical Categories:

Blue Collar
White Collar
Nerd
Asshole
Slut
Redneck
Conservative
Liberal
Black
White
Asian
LGBT
Latin
Anonymous

Native American
Player
Jock
Bitch
Performer
Celebrity
Star
User
Loser
Controller
Politician
Wannabe
Jerk
Stud
Gonnabe
Was
If I Had Only
Lost
Etc.

The list is longer.

And they're all part of the....

American Social Role Hierarchy:

Famous
Rich
Wealthy
Upper Middle Class
Middle Class
Lower Middle Class
Poor
Youth
Middle Age
Elderly
Old
Too Old To Matter
Homeless
Mentally Disturbed
Buried

Which means there are

American Spiritual Characteristics:

Spiritual Integrity
Pretend Spiritual Integrity
Spiritual Hustling
Superior Mental and Physical Health
Messed Up Mind
Messed Up Body

Both
Honest
Liar
Greedy
Stingy
Generous
Stubborn
Prayerful
Critical
Hypocritical
Uptight
Playful
Wishing & Hopeful
Whatever
Screw It
Ditch

Consider:

In America, there are basically two types of cultural motion: horizontal and lateral.

Horizontality signifies same ol', same ol', even if it brings wealth.

Laterality signifies distraction and procrastination.

Both directions lack much verticality, progress.

Verticality implies *'up'*….indicative of growth, self-transcendence, self-alteration….maturing.

So....

Growing up is more difficult than developing laterally or horizontally.

The American Trance generally implies:
'You're on your own'.
'Family is second to success.
'Pursue your dreams but be practical'.
'Wealth is a good goal'.
'The rich run the show'.
'Stand out, win *something*'.
'Being ordinary is a bummer'.
'Anger, arguing, emotional violence, physical and verbal abuse, flipping fingers, and swearing, are normal'.
'Love is a feeling'.
'Justice is blind'.
'Everything happens for a reason'.
'What goes around comes around'.
'It wasn't meant to be'....etc.

This denotes the
American Trance **Priorities**:

Money
Entertainment
Sex
Possessions
Success

Winning
Believe
Appearance

And the

American Trance **Secondary Priorities**:

Personal Health
Savings

Connected to
American Trance **Small Obligatory Priorities**:

Humanitarianism
Health Care
Social Welfare
Children & Education

And the
American Trance **Least Important Priorities**:

Thinking
Civics
Military Service
Honesty
Maturing completely
Art
The Environment
Learning

All of which cause

Some Dominant Cultural Result Facts:

- American maturity is an oxymoron.
- Children are a precious burden.
- Argue rather than discuss.
- Lie if it works for you.
- If it feels good, do it.
- God is boring.
- Make money.
- Have fun.
- Get laid.
- Win.

Accompanying those facts:

- The Movie Theatre, Television Screen, Sports Arena, Race Track, Concert Location, Toy Store, Social Media, and the Human Ear have replaced houses of worship.
    &
    The Lens has replaced the eye and is closing in on the I.
- Fans are *the* congregations.

- American Devotion is primarily for *living* gods. American gods and goddesses are The Modern American Actor.
- America is a costume culture, physically and mentally, because so many Americans tend to live as though looked at and judged….as if to say worth is measurable and measured….in a glance.

That means personal security so often is sustained by appearance, possessions, fashions, hairs, symbols, styles, and idiosyncratic imitations of types….done for some degree of Cool. It's social acting.

So what's the point?

The point is, role-playing and personal 'style' are pervasive from the White House to the pulpit, from corporate to the courts, from farms and ranches, and from the streets to prisons to homes to beds. It's part of the American Way.

The only place there is no role-playing is in a crib.

To reiterate:

The influence of TMAA is a *phenomenon of under-estimated importance*.

That importance is increasing. It points to another salient characteristic of the current American

Trance—inventions that unite earthly and divine as replacements for losses of traditional worship practices and objects of devotion.

Consider....

- ✦ We all seek peace through seeking how to rhyme with who we are through what we do.

We try to find the kinds of intimacy that rhymes us so we can become a fuller rhyme—grow. Otherwise, we're less rhymed: unhappy, troubled, confused, discouraged, in the blues, edgy, lost, regretful, and maybe dangerous. The goal of human creativity is deeply meaningful self-completion. It's a great joy to say 'I rhyme with I'.

- ✦ American culture encourages the creative by reinforcing mantra-statements:
  follow your dreams
  follow your heart
  follow your bliss
  sacrifice
  work
      &
  endure
  pursue
  to get to 'over the rainbow'....

So
'if you love it, do it'....
and
'don't give up'....

Which means:

If you're gripped by a conviction of who you are and who you can become, then all you have to do is believe, do the work and one day you'll make it—you'll answer Dorothy's question 'Why, oh why, can't I?'

Americology says 'you can, you can, you can'.

If you're a seeker and a dreamer and you hang in there, you will answer 'I will, I will, I will' until you can sing 'I did, I did, I did'.

That's basically how the logic and effort of American success-thinking works.

And it has validity up to a point.

Related to that....

TMAA 'inspires' the dreams of thousands of teenagers annually in sports, music, singing, dancing, and acting....

That means....

American Youth has beautifully wild urges to enjoy open-ended desire creatively.

They're not reaching for the *practical*.

They're reaching for the practical through the *personal* as part of an intuitively creative search that eventually *will* 'make sense' of becoming a self…it'll all rhyme.

Those wild urges must be acknowledged and encouraged for what they are—natural.

But American Education doesn't dig education, kids, and the arts, really dig them. They have to be fought for.

Crazy.

And related to that….

Great teaching in any field inspires students to pursue living with accurate aim, joy of effort, and standards of excellence requiring discipline, thoroughness, questions, and *confidence*.

So, Typical American Education has to be partially transcended so creativity and confidence can be included as core issues for self-integrations that indicate the essence of what personal success is all about.

But

American Education, like all of America, is competitive and extrinsically oriented: largely focused on external evidence of *accomplishment*—'winning'—rather than on the internal search for an affinity that will lead to *achievement* beyond but inclusive of accomplishments and winning.

A lot of nurtured genius in America is lost because a lot of kids don't have the liberty—the options—to get inside the arena to seek, find, begin to grow into personal artistry in any field, and create a self-portrait that blends work, living, and love into meanings that promote working, living, and loving.

A lotta kids never get to rhyme that way.

Unarguable conclusion: because kids aren't fully appreciated and, therefore, more deeply important to America, their education isn't either.

—The Student Part—

American youths tend not to fully understand patience and labor as buddies that are part of completing a dream pursuit. Many students want to get rollin' right away, right now, and pick up the learning pieces as they go. That's partially valid because there's only so much you can pick up in the classroom.

The most and the best you can pick up in classes are reliable seeds—the basics of thinking and doing—for a lifetime of planting, growing, and harvesting.

If you've ever planted a seed, patience rules. Water as needed and wait....be consistent. And know, each variety of seed is different....adapt to *it* so you can provide what sustains growth. When that's done, the growth of the seed grows you.

It's obvious, as stated, that:

All persons are creative
> But
> Very few persons can make *great art* in any field
> And
> Art isn't confined to 'the arts'.

Students of acting should be very clear about identifying with the work and pleasure of acting rather than with the image of being an actor/actress.

Thoughts:

You never stop being a virgin. Development, however, can and does stop in many folks long before dying.
> &

Making magic (the good) from your humanness is the artistry of living and loving. Not 'to make' the good is to die.
> &

Young children cannot play a social role. All they can do is play.
> &

Great persons are great lights.

Great artists work only for light.
Children are the light.
Light is truth.
Truth in 'light' is beauty.
All children bring light naturally.
They bring it to us.
That's why they're beautiful.
   &

If we do not live for light, we do not live fully; we just cope, adapt, adjust, and feel shade as the absence of what could have been brighter if only we'd 'seen the light' sooner.

Call it regret.

Side note:

Many persons think, talk, and read about *success*.

And many folks talk about *personal success* in contrast to financial success.

If you're able to develop both genuinely, you'll become philanthropic.

Philanthropy is not related only to money. But money helps because giving money wisely *helps*.

The greatest philanthropists receive more than they can ever give.

The greatest philanthropists give what is theirs to give.

The greatest humans give beyond what they can give.

This is the beauty of sacrifice that guarantees no loss, no pain, no regret. Sacrifice is a good word, often misunderstood.

You have to be mature, however, to offer sacrifice generously.

Or a child.

Back to acting....

Genuine receptivity is the activity of authentic generosity.

That's how living and any artistic acting experience work best.

All acting is centered on multiple relationships. If any of the primary relationships are deficient, there's imbalance. Just like living.

The premiere relationship for the actor/actress is script. Words. The better the writer, the more complete, complex, and rewarding is the journey for the actor, unless there's a problem with other cast members, time, organization, or a director.

Considering some of the obvious....

- Many actors and teachers of acting like to think of acting as an art form. Why?

Is acting an art form?
Yes and no.

+ The only *form* to acting is the basic three-way contract that binds script to actor, actor to actor, and actors to audience.

However….this tri-unity usually requires a director whose job is to facilitate and coordinate all creative interactions with maximum clarity and efficiency for maximum communicative effect.

This means the entire 'show' must pass through the director *empathically* and creatively many times—in discussions with all persons involved, in nearly all rehearsals, and during the shooting of a film, or until the opening night of a play.

So:

+ Ultimately, to make acting live *artistically* is the primary goal of all basic playwriting, screenwriting, directing, and acting.

+ Basic acting believability is analogous to having a conversation with a friend during a meal in a café or restaurant. The friends can sense whether the folks at a nearby table are interested. If so, the friends can *dramatize*—shape and edit everything spontaneously to sustain audience interest and understanding. And they do this without letting it be perceived that 'it's all an act'. They make it *believable* and progressively informative based on a tension-premise. They know the 'audience' at the other table is a resource and the final recipient....so they create a *complete* illusion of 'living', out of which comes the 'art' of giving in acting and in dance, singing, opera, musicianing, composing, writing, architecting, painting, sculpting, journaling.... anyone engaged in substantive creativity.

So, to backtrack a little: what is....

BASIC ACTING....

Ever bake a cake?

Takes basic ingredients.

Add too much or too little of one, or leave one out, then yeah it's still a cake and it may look like a cake but it isn't *complete*. And if it's the cake you've always made, then you can't sense anything's missing, that it's incomplete. Someone who knows more about cakes has to tell you what's missing. Either you accept the comments and redo your recipe or you don't. If you accept the comments, you try to trust who's telling you, then try out the suggestion. If that person doesn't really know how to tell you so you 'get it', you either keep going…or you look for someone else who's supposed to know what they're talking about, or you continue doing what you've always done. Or you quit.

Extend the analogy to acting and teaching.
What are the basic 'ingredients' *essential* for acting, for teaching?

For acting

They are:

- Self
- Language
- Make-believe
- Others
- Purpose
- Doing

The combined interrelatedness and interactions of those 'ingredients' are what makes acting basic because the ingredients are the essentials of how we all live.

If you're a young actor/actress trying to understand this and figure how to get it going in a balanced way, remember, the ingredients are yours to assemble, so do it your way. Just make sure they're all in the mix and you don't overcook or undercook—overdo, underdo.

Takes time to get it *right*, get it *your* way right, get it *artistically* right....and keep it balanced.

Ultimately, that's what makes acting *good*
    &
What makes acting great?

The only answer is sustained *completeness*
    Because
Completely complete in continuity is the greatness of all great artistry.

Teaching:

The basis of all good teaching and teaching acting must be:

- first, *reduce ignorance* creatively
- second, *enhance the enjoyment of learning* creatively
- third, *nurture confidence creatively*
- fourth, do all three from the get go.

Yes, *acting **is** living*. That's the essence of the artistry of acting. Anything less is acting with less artistry.

How humans and living are understood by a teacher shapes how thoroughly, openly, accurately, flexibly, and actually that teacher will teach living into the training/study of acting.

Solid teachers get that.

Lesser teachers tend to emphasize narrower, personalized versions of teaching, and often are impatient, excessively analytical, intensely checked out, plain checked out, controllers, idealists, sentimentalists, arrogant, and/or deeply in habit.

This starves learning.

Bottom lines are:

- Every essential class in an acting curriculum *is an acting class.*
- Every teacher should have an experiential clarity about the unity of all areas of emphases pertinent to acting.

Why?

Because it makes learning more local—personal to the student rather than generally reflective of a narrower 'approach', 'theory', or 'philosophy' that homogenizes students by asking them to graft self on to a teacher's way of teaching.

- The teacher needs to adapt wholly to the individual and find ways to communicate the basics effectively, sensitively, and patiently.
- Solid teachers in any field always adapt completely to individual students, one by one, and

bring to each student opportunities to experience more complete awareness of the 'ingredients'.

+ Solid teachers in any field know explanations are necessary but only if they're *creatively valid*—arousing imagination first, understanding second by guiding the doing creatively so the talking matters more.

So:

What's important in early stages of study/training for acting is the nurturing of raw willingness expertly guided toward confidence that enhances make-believe for the unity of self and yes....as both slowly merge *into* the demands of scripted language and a director.

So:

Believability and 'your way' of doing acting are how the eye of the 'I' eventually will mark your effort with uniqueness. This eliminates imitation and gives rise to individuation: from identity as actor/actress to identifying self with acting and through acting right beside truly successful living for the good.

So, as stated:

+ The make-believe of acting relies totally on nurturing imagination for actual encounters—

living—with living *persons* also in make-believe, not just 'in character'.

+ Brain functioning in acting must basically occur like it does in daily living.
+ To counter analytical creativity—crafting an effort—perhaps it's helpful to think of imagination as a sidekick you talk to. If you talk too much, too little, or too vaguely, imagination yawns and doesn't get it. Tunes out. Then you tune out creatively and end up thinking your way through a process, assembling conclusions you duplicate/imitate while supplying appropriate feelings and behavior. That's shallow acting.

Always easy to spot.
Lot of it around.
So....

+ Actors/actresses must learn effective ways of *self-talk* that facilitate specific imaginative arousal and the excitement of an accurate *impulse* to do.

No impulse, nothing left but faking it dramatically to compensate for what's missing genuinely. That can become a habit that leads to slickness stylized and refined.

+ Impulse self-talk is the ignition key. If it's a valid key, it always works, gets the engine running for what's possible all the way to let's do it and, finally, yeah, it's on! That's what little kids do, and they do it *right now*.

Impulse combined with mastery, the maturity of playing simply, generously, and genuinely in superb continuity without extra tension are the core of genius.

Without the ignition key/self-talk slang in acting, there's only:

Analysis and
The Glossary and
Boredom rationalized
Accompanied by
Endless Talk
Questions & Perplexity, counterproductive habits, and the staleness of fake acting
related to
What should be free, spontaneous, responsible, compellingly honest, thorough, and….

- ✦ Basically, deeply fun. Professionally, sometimes that fun is difficult to generate.
- ✦ Very early, during the personal engagement phase permitting the 'I live' experience of the creative impulse, the 'you live too' factor must be built firmly into any instruction of acting:

I to you, you to me....*we*. You and me, not our characters.

Then do what little kids do—play deeper into playing *together*, with full acceptance of everything to be explored to discover more, more, more. That's creative study in any role, in any material for acting, at any age.

In daily living, we pay very close attention to anyone when we *need* something: an apology, a yes, a no, a maybe, consolation, advice, forgiveness, a thank you, acceptance, money, an explanation, a head nod, closeness, clarity, etc. Otherwise, we're in courteous chatter patterns because the other person doesn't matter that much.

Actors/actresses often do chatter patterns when acting and don't know it because feeling, 'character', and self have largely eclipsed relationship, dependency, sensitivity to others, vulnerability, and and other aspects of artistic integrity.

So, what are the basic questions (apart from the question of 'character') for acting through imagination?

They are:

Who am I?
What's the writer asking me to *feel?*

What does that feeling make me *need?*
What does that need make me *do?*
What's the *ideal result* of my effort?
What's going on *in the other person* while I'm talking?

Answer the questions directly and simply, always in your own slang, so your imagination/mind can grasp the experience of each answer as *the urge to **do**,* relate, think and play.

Simple, slang answers should always trigger clarity, arousal, engagement—personally and interpersonally—and endeavor:

Living with *purpose* through *action.*

A relationship analogy:

Playing tennis….

When you serve, you're completely dependent on the other player for continuity; how that will occur is familiar and defined by the sport but actual game actions are completely unpredictable.

You know how you feel and what you *need* and need to *do*—you know what's genuinely *driving* you, and you go for the desired result, right to the end. Your focus is primarily on the other player's responses to what you do with the ball. So you continuously adapt and pay real close attention to what you receive and what you need to do next. The more talent you have and the more you play, the more perceptive, artistic, nuanced, and complete is your technique.

So….it's back and forth, over and over, each player zeroed in on what's going on and what to do next.

It's completely spontaneous—*discovered*—but completely guided by a mutual dependency of *relationship* and driven *need* completed moment to moment through *doing:* living related to aim, purpose, and conclusion without excess tension.

Acting should be the same. Always.

Final point:
Instead of a ball, actors use….

Language….

Words are the extension of all that precedes and causes them,
   & therefore
They're the link from self to other, even in silence.
In this sense, humans are language
Because
Spoken language, one way or another, contains the entire human: his/her history, environment, preoccupations, and psychology.

So....

Spoken language emerges from a 'world' and travels toward the 'world' of another human or humans. It attempts to penetrate the other world and guide it, moment by moment.

So....

For acting, increased sensitivity to language is the first step toward basic *acting artistry* that eventually will include what is called 'character'.

When seeing any highly respected actor/actress/singer, rapper, or comedian whose sensitivity to the nuances of experience that all well-written language is, we witness how thought, feeling, meaning, and purpose cause refined clarity and poise, and solid, purposeful artistry.

So....

Sensitivity to language and humans causes us to listen closely, to see more fully, to understand—know what's going on in a person while it's going on.

Animals and small children live this way, in touch with what's going on with what interests them 'in the moment'. They're available....poised selectively *within* what we call time as the 'now'.

But for the beginning actor/actress, poise can only be a goal. Scripts first must be used to learn the basics of acting.

When the basics are adequately coordinated, the actor/actress can slowly begin to serve scripts and take more demanding instruction and direction, knowingly and responsibly.

Until that time, all scripted material must be used to enhance acting. That means take the full pressure off of serving the material. Use the material to explore how to act. It's a mistake to ask beginning actors to address the script fully.

So....

The entire early learning experience for young actor/actress must be centered *first* on believability and relationship. If that's not the case, there can be no additional demands made of a student.

Believability begins when the fullness of 'be' precedes 'do'. That's the basis for 'being in the moment' in relationship.

No be, no living. Just less complete acting.

Back to language:

It's not how language is spoken, but the interactive causes of speaking that must be empathically intuited rather than analytically supplied through familiar patterns and turned-on emotion.

The opportunity language brings is to learn how to become intuitively clearer, more like actual living.

The 'how' of this clarity in relation to why, however, shifts nearly all the time because all words are not synonyms.

It's very easy to pattern dialogue at the expense of individual words where the nuances wait to be opened and offered.

Nevertheless....

The 'why' has become the basis for excessive thinking analysis in contrast to what I'm discussing—*the priority of imaginative analysis* from which honest, creative analysis can occur.

Obviously, there's an overlap. Imagination always includes thinking/receiving as a factor accompanying playing. The difference is one of emphasis and surrender.

It's very easy to be attracted to thought analysis at the expense of imaginative analysis. Thought analysis promises control.

About the word 'character'....

Which I've placed in quotes throughout this book because it's a major concept in all talk about acting.

What is it?

It's a reference to a written person to be converted by actor/actress from script into make-believe and living interactions.

For the actor/actress, it's the basis for 'look who I get to be' and 'what I get to do'.

Typically, for completeness, 'character' often requires varying kinds of research, inquiry, photos, recordings, conversations and anything else that facilitates complete clarity, definition, familiarity, and accuracy.

Again, this 'process' usually will be tilted in one of two directions:

Toward the analytical, crafting a performance....
or
Toward the imaginative and portraiture.

Portraiture for acting is the ultimate invitation.
Portraiture is essence revealed.
Not so in performance.

So consider:

✦ We all know the hardest task in human relations is to know another person.

✦ Words, one way or another, always provide the basis for lasting impressions of the world, self, and another human....words supply the clues, what we all can sense is present, because we're looking to see, to know, to determine, to *decide* about another human being so we know where we stand, what to expect, and what to do.

✦ If 'character' does not include all of this sensitively and appropriately—artistically—then character is more easily defined through skilled behavior in a clearly established 'personality/behavior mood-mode' completed through costume, attitude, and intensified feeling that carries language along for the ride. Sensitivity and vulnerability are diminished.

This tends to exclude other actors in specific ways and eliminate the subtle shifts that occur continuously in a *human* world.

It is those subtle shifts of internal awareness that must be intuited by the actor/actress continuously for portraiture to emerge.

Otherwise, as stated, acted language is generalized into intense lump statements that level it to melodrama and familiar patterns adamantly spoken.

In American Acting, one pattern dominates.

✦ Patterning carries over into *dialects*. A lotta folks can do accents flawlessly. To that they add the rest of what they do to secure the conviction of solid acting.

But....

A dialect/accent is a shared way of speaking by folks from another region or country. It's derived from local and cultural rhythms, symbols, thinking, doing, and living. There's history in it.

So, yes....

Dialects are a different way of speaking
    &
Either you have an affinity for dialects or not.

However,

Differences in speaking (rhythm, tone, intonation patterns, and syllabic/phonemic nuances) denote cultural differences that shape and perpetuate ways of thinking—the living mentality of a group.

To imaginatively grasp that way of 'living' and seeing is the core of how to develop a dialect in acting so spoken language retains its integrity and flow.

And this is where it becomes difficult for persons (actor/actress) to do dialect work more completely, even though the mechanics may be flawless.

So....

In the best dialect/accent work culture, disposition, and world view are imaginatively and accurately grasped—perceived. They unite rhythmically and authentically, and cause increased clarity and fun of *other-being-ness*....a changed self rather than a projected self....which takes us....

Back to character:

Character always is 'living' in a different way.
Light character is called stereotype. Imitation.
However,
Things shift from surface lightness and predictable behavior and gestures when a student is asked to do a stereotype with depth, fullness....do a full-on human, sincerely.

That's one way to knock on the door to portraiture.

Find the human, a different kind of you. Do it completely, imaginatively. Then do language in genuine relationship.

To reiterate:

+ Basic reading for acting means reading sensitively and vulnerably to receive experience in the form of words to be spoken in ways that contain all the experience a good writer wrote.

+ Basic reading for acting should occur as though listening to a story or watching something of great personal interest....no agenda other than to *see into,* receive openly, react, and form impressions freely, spontaneously.

✦ This entire effort, if done imaginatively, is the best way to study script and complete a role because it leads to fresh arousal and insights that live....

from self to
make-believe identity/self
in
relationships
and with
language
that is
structured
for
discovery
of
doing
that is
purposeful, accurate, increasingly complete
and
fun: **play**.

How all of this is actually done varies from person to person, project to project. But in all solid acting, imaginative inquiry and arousal are done creatively

The Happy Castle

rather than as an effort to 'break down' a script then reassemble the bits cognitively and logically—crafting a performance instead of making a portrait.

So....

Build it up, don't break it down.

Woo it sincerely, patiently, humbly, excitedly, knowledgeably.

Related to all that, as you know....

A Writer is a container.
A Script is a container.
The Actor is a container.
The Director is a container.
The Venue is a container.
So....

All persons connected to the development, producing, marketing, and distribution of the container that's for sale are also containers—they give to the 'Big Container', the final product, so it can be sold to the ultimate, final container called An Audience.

Related to that in a much smaller but truly grand way:

My granddaughter, Vivienne, is a six year old container. She chooses little containers called books and waits for me to open them, make them live so she can talk/play while I read/play.

I love reading to/with/for her because I get to play into language with some magic called 'story time'....I get to see into the sweet beauty of a child's mind and spirit dancing with and into words and ideas, into learning, learning how to fly words while I supply some wind and direction for a little unpredictable soaring.

&

For me, that's what art and living is all about: live to love to live to do and give....toward the possible, all wrapped in

Basics
Artistry
Poise
Curiosity
Mastery
Humility
Enjoyment
Completeness

The Happy Castle

Moving right along....in summary:

- ✦ Actors do acting because of who and what influenced them.
- ✦ Acting is too simple and natural for any kind of theory. Theory is theoretical. Acting is actual.
- ✦ The teaching of acting requires an environment for learning how to duplicate living, but doing it *artistically*....edited to essentials and balanced specificities.

So:

A Master Teacher of Acting must know, study, learn, and be able to demonstrate and integrate:

Acting
Writing
Voicing
Moving
Directing
Noting

On the other hand....

American acting and teaching do not require this wide range of expertise
    Because

American acting is adequate for American audiences, for most directors and producers, and for the actor/actress.

Mastery is largely irrelevant.

Side note:

Some acting teachers use the words intent, intention. Therefore, teachers often ask students 'What do you want?' or 'What's your intention?' related to a scene, monologue, or improvisation.

To clarify:

Intent/want is conation related to future activity. Want and intent permit the alternative to what is wanted.

For example, if you say:

I want to get in shape.
I want to go to Hawaii.
I want to lose weight.
I want to be an actor....

That's different than saying

I'm going to get in shape.
I'm going to Hawaii.
I'm going to lose weight.
I'm going to be an actor/actress....

'Want/intent' mean I'd like to but....

'Going to' is full-on commitment: no alternative, no negotiation—a more complete statement of drive and goal.

The psychology of the two statements is similar but qualitatively different.

Anyway, to continue summarizing:

- The job of actors is to bring *substance* (the complex actuality of living) to expression.
- If substance is not written into the language, then the language is not substantial. It becomes patterned melodrama in motion toward predictable conclusions.
- When movies and television programs are talky, it's 'serious' and tends to lose viewers

Americans don't like to listen for long.
So....
Talky movies are usually considered boring.
&

- That's why theatre—except musicals—isn't that popular in America.

Musicals entertain. Plays typically don't.

Years ago, I sat in on L.A. undergraduate auditions in South Central Los Angeles. They were sponsored by the Yale School of Drama for teens who wanted to act. The turnout was overwhelming. And so was the talent….completely uneducated and raw, beautiful and moving. *Hungry*. The kind of hunger that is enviable and luminous: driven.

Person after person acted….did Shakespeare without knowing about it, begged to act a personal poem, tried to stay and talk, sing a song….why? Because (and I cry at the memory) they were filled with jubilant *desire* confined within desperate beauty entangled in the morass of poverty and impoverishment preventing their beauty from being heard, seen, and honored. But that morning they had a chance. They were struggling to be free enough to take the *chance* and fly it over a rainbow.

They did, for a few divine minutes.

Their beauty taught me.

—Back To America—

To reiterate:

1. *American Melodrama* appeals because it unites actions and themes with principles and values centered on juxtaposing good and evil so the

triumph of the good happens. This also occurs in comedies.
2. *American Melodrama,* particularly in television and film, is a key cultural guardian of love, justice, and safety.
3. Repeated contact with melodrama is essential for the cohesiveness of American Identity, American Stability, and for continued success in business.
4. *Entertainment* is *the* major American stabilizer—

It is:

Movies
Television
Video Games
Audiovisual Technology
Wireless Technology
Computers
Music & Songs
Social Media
Gambling
Pro Wrestling
Plays
Sports
Vehicles
Dance
Shopping Malls
Amazon

Cars & Racing
Motorcycles
Pornography
Fashion
Amusement

The most important Personal Medium is Music & Song.

The most important Cultural Mediums are The Movie and the Internet/Television.

The most important American Cultural Person is TMAA.

There is another set of American containers called:

Rules
Laws
Work
Marriage
Divorce
Competition
Win
Lose
Dream
Family
Money
Right

Disease
Guilt
Wrong
Lie
Poverty
Depression
Ordinary
Reality
Racism
Religion
Anxiety
Compromise
Prison
Doubt
Distrust
Denial
Ethics
Morality
Vanity

Love and death are not containers.
They change us....into receivers.

In addition....

Irrespective of the few million Americans who truly champion the ideals of love, charity, and compassion, one grisly fact remains—America spiritually and financially places folks in one of three categories:

important
functionaries
unimportant

So....Prominent American Bottom Lines are:

If it's not cost effective, it's not worth implementing.
Don't waste money on unimportant persons.
Lose humans, keep money, make money.
Lose humans, keep things, make money.
Neglect children....oh well.

Afterthought fragments:

Perhaps, the male artist is a woman's heart with a man's temperament....

The female artist is a woman's temperament with a man's heart.

America is deeply available in a multiplicity of resources:

in old, unused libraries
in old persons' stories
in their eyes and hands

&

in the events that have given this nation its best traits and concerns, accomplishments, achievements, and hopes for the future....

&

in the young.

But....

The dynamics of this nation may produce its endgame minus the game....because....

Love for humans lasts as long as it is pursued.

A tiny, short, personal note:

When I was in my early twenties, I wanted to be one of the best actors on the planet.

So I took steps:

April 1965

Got drafted.

Took a physical at the Induction Center for the military.

Got reclassified due to injuries.

Spoke to Sir Tyrone Guthrie.

August, graduated with a B.A. in Humanities; University of Minnesota.

Got a ride to L.A. to say goodbye to broken parents.

Got a ride to Iowa.
Made it to NYC.

September 1965

Took a midnight last-ride alone on the front of The Cyclone rickety wood roller coaster at Coney Island.

Slept with a girl in Brooklyn.

Sept. 8th, early a.m., boarded Castel Felice, an older, Italian ship. Left America....passed the Statue of Liberty while talking to a young man, trench coat, curly long hair....named Mario Savio, leader of the Free Speech Movement centered in Berkeley.

Talked a lot. He was hooked in. I was ignorant. Both on our way to London. He was on his way to Oxford....I think that's what he said....tired, preoccupied, passionate, tense, somewhat disillusioned, searching, and trying to make sense of it all. In my own way, so was I.

Had about a hundred bucks in my pocket, no way home.

Eleven day voyage. Dieppe, Ostend, Southampton.

Auditioned for The Central School of Speech and Drama five days before school started. Late afternoon, dark, rainy; one slot open. Last person to be told. The answer was yes.

The Happy Castle

Went wild; had enough for a roundtrip to Paris; went that night on the overnight train and ferry.

Around 8 a.m.—Gare St. Lazare.

Marveled that everyone spoke French. Duh.

Became a student of acting.

Lived hard for three years as in mostly homeless and sometimes not.

Studied everything. Stole food, worked odd-jobs, hitch-hiked everywhere. Saw the underbelly and art of Europe five times. Went to North Africa. Experienced existential beauties on foreign soil while looking for affirmations of my existence. It happened more than once. There's a whole lot more to this adventure....it all led to:

June 1968....

Landed in NYC.

'Began a career' at the same time I was really changing as a person.

Got work and an important agent quickly.

Got a tiny part in a major film with an unknown named Jon Voight and another guy I'd barely heard of....Dustin Hoffman.

Part was cut.

Went bicoastal.

But I was changing.

After a run-in of 'say one thing, do another' with a fellow named Steve McQueen, I felt a Classic Hollywood Shock....commonly called a lie. It was real hard. I was naïve but principled. My word has always been my bond. That's what I learned in Wyoming. You give your word, you keep it. I learned a lotta folks don't live that way.

And I was changing.

Fall....1969

Gave a roast-beef sandwich with a ring in it to a young lady I'd met in Honolulu when I quit college.

Got married.

Auditioned.

Quit acting—

Told my agent I quit and wouldn't be back. His jaw dropped. Within a month I got offers for a series and other work. But I was clear.

Went to work in a Beverly Hills clothing store. Hated it. Lasted two months. Quit. Started refinishing furniture on a vacant lot.

Spring '70....

Went to work for an antique store.

Made an impulse phone-call to a local university. Asked if there was a teaching position in the Theater Dept. There was. I interviewed. Several world-class names on my short resume and enough work done. Got the job.

Three courses: movement, voice, and acting.

Never taught a day in my life.

But...

I wanted to teach. And I wanted to try to learn how to think and write better.

I didn't understand that I also needed to learn how to love better; not more deeply, but more openly as in more completely—the intimately shared, sensitive, trusting version.

I didn't understand much about that because I'd not come from a home of love.

Nevertheless....

Became a father. Twice. Yay! Loved every minute of it; still do.

But

Years later, got a divorce. Very painful. Worse for my daughters. Tried to hold them up to the sun everyday. They are a gift to me and my gift to this world; I honor them daily.

But I made some mistakes. Ignorant.

Wanted to learn every aspect of acting. Told myself, 'If I ever return to acting, the only reason I won't get the job is because I don't look right'.

Wanted to learn it all. Still *hungry*. Determined.

But….I was really changing.
So….
Became a teacher/coach of it all and kept on studying—went to Graduate School.

Never taught what I couldn't do. How well I could do it all, who knows? But I could do it. I knew I could put it on the line anywhere, anytime. A few times I had to do that. Demonstrate.

Had keep on learning how to do it better.
Kept on training/studying on my own, working out, and truckin'.

Fast forward forty years:

I'm sitting in this old Wyoming cabin, 11 p.m.
10 degrees outside. Wind.
Shoveled snow *again*. Quarter mile of it, 12 feet wide. T-shirt, cowboy hat, bandana around my mouth. I worked it, hard and fast. Defiant. And singing. Not the first time.

A thought:

The slow proliferation of diminished regard for beauty is the basis for the contemporary deformity of art.

A fact:

That may not concern you.

Homage To African-American Creativity

To my knowledge, there is no other people on the planet able to match the expressive depth of freedom present in the African-American.

By depth I mean this: freedom occurs *actually* at the very moment a choice is made. All else precedes a moment of choice.

Call the moment of choice the depth and definition of *now;* and call choice the home of courage.

For the African-American, their only continuous, genuine possession has been *now*.

Now is a very demanding possession because to live it you have to live *inside* the freedom of it and make it count.

The Happy Castle

The African-American has done that, lived the now into the realm of genius.

The collective history of the African-American is centered on now because regular time has been and, in various ways, continues to be unavailable and precariously unpredictable.

For the African-American, the only choice has become *within* now: live in spite of not being able to live.

Freedom is related to liberty.
Liberty is a person's range of options.
All liberty was taken from the African-American.
Yet
No force on earth has dislodged African-American freedom.

In this sense, the African-American has transcended freedom.

That means:

+ Living without being able to live has become the verticality of African-American creativity—a fusion of time and being beyond the savagery of those who, then and now, tolerate, hate, and attack the African-American.

Why does that occur?

Homage to African-American Creativity

Because the African American has what this nation has not—an unbreakable holiness of spirit....

That means the African American cannot be destroyed.

Only killed.

African-American beauty and spirit are unequalled anywhere in America.

African-American creativity is without equal anywhere in America.

African-American perseverance is living evidence of the bible's great hymn and promise in the final verse of Romans 8.

White folks *often* sense the presence of those facts, and they are so *often* enviously mesmerized by the African-American identity as a living cultural force that cannot be vanquished. That identity is a highly developed sense of humor, spontaneous love, and generosity combined *within a way to live* while continuing to strive against exclusion.

The African-American has changed America.

The African-American has given their people to America.

The African-American has enriched every area of human endeavor in America and inspired Americans of all hues to match the excellence of African-American achievements and the depth of African-American devotion to love.

Disrespect and hatred for the African-American has fueled genius *in* the African-American.

African-American genius has *offered* to the world its *jewels*.

America does not understand *how* the jewels are *made*.

Only the African-American knows how that occurs, from what, and why.

The African-American has learned *how* to move through a locked door for which there is no key or handle.

The African-American has learned *how* make beauty.

The African-American has learned *how* to carry heavy weight on a broken back, how to heal the broken back, then carry even more weight....and still offer, still share, still laugh.

Therefore....

The African-American is a mystery for most white persons. That mystery fascinates and alienates

Because

No white person can enter the world of the African- American except socially....and partially through marriage. The remainder of the African-American world is not available to whites, not even

Homage to African-American Creativity

through empathy, compassion, observation, deep friendship, or respect....

Because

The white person has not learned how to do what the African-American has done and is doing.

And African-Americans do it in ways the white person will never know because the white person is not African-American and has not been challenged to survive on one heartbeat a day.

The white person's home is a house.
The African-American has a home beyond a house.
White persons sense this.
The home of the African-American is in spirit: in the immediacy of time appreciated and endured, in the pure now where celebration of now is and must remain instantaneous—*with* & *in* the word....God.

The African-American belongs, in spite of not belonging.

The African-American celebrates, in spite of not belonging.

The African-American creates from nothing that which is eternal.

African-American contributions to America have given full voice to white culture and, ironically, is releasing America from its white, personal prison.

The African-American carries the key to this nation's freedom because....

The African-American carries the Sun, translates its music, writes its books and lyrics on air, and reaches out with truth's moving beauty, moving in eyes that carry the history of how humankind has failed to love....eyes that wait and watch, wait for America to read that history and learn lyrics of the Sun.

The African-American did not, has not, and will not try to dodge, deny, or escape from history.

The African-American will continue to mark history and the cosmos with the mark of that unbreakable....holiness of spirit.

* * *

What about Latin, Asian, Biracial, and the Native-Americans? Where is their place in The Happy Castle?

This I *know*....

The white diamond is not the most important gem because there is no most important gem. There are only gem-buying habits. Jewels of all hues have equal value.

If you are a gem with a hue other than white diamond, and you are deeply talented and uncut, then _learn learn learn_ so when you choose to let your light shine, you will be brilliantly visible and equally irresistible.

You _will_ work.

What's Going On & What's Next

Well, a lot's going on in America and around the world.

Big time.

In America, all structures are shifting.
TMAA is part of those structures....

FOR THE TMAA GENTS:

There will continue to be the ongoing American Mix of virility, rebellion, crudeness, kickass toughness, subdued humor, humility and mild arrogance mixed with variations of indifference and self-styled confidence—the acting tatts based on Brando's designs because....as you know....

He knocked acting up.
Became the father.
And the godfather.

The Happy Castle

FOR THE TMAA LADIES:

The war for equality is on.
They're winning.
They will win.

Consider, after 1960 in America:

JFK was shot.
Dr. King was shot.
Medgar Evers was shot.
The Black Panthers rose nobly and were destroyed.
RFK was shot.
Malcolm X was shot.
Vietnam was a bust.
Beatniks wrote.
Hippies danced and sang.
Native Americans held on.
Comedy broke free.
Cassius Clay became Muhammad Ali.
Nixon was a bust.
Reagan was shot.
Computer World was born.
Rap was born.
Education was bought.
Mt. Porn erupted.
More laws were bought.
John Lennon was shot.
The NRA became political.

Greed won.
Civil rights laws were passed.
Politics began to be a glaring Gathering of Fools.
Lobbying provided a trough.
Gangs evolved.
Drugs hit the scene.
Megachurches and televangelists began pimping the Bible.
Facts became more confused with truth.
Arbitrary thinking sought the throne and began shaping a crown to fit the misshapenness.
&
The legacy of ignorance, negligence, and arrogance increased.
We see the results of that fact throughout earth's natural environments and its species as they, one by one, like old sunflowers, droop into passing.
Because of us. Perhaps to include us.

And today:

Kids in cities continue to be shot.
Racism has nowhere to hide because of The Lens.
Immaturity is rampant.
Drugs are rampant.
Confusion is rampant.
Trust is a derelict.

Politicians reveal themselves in corners fucking their lies.

Religion wanders in its narrowness and struggles to breathe.

Dreamers dream. Seekers seek. Humans strive.

Americans are crying out because of growing pains.

The world wriggles, wars, gropes in fear and blame, and binges on the grapes of wrath.

So....

With all that's going on today, what's actually happening in American acting....?

Part of the answers are obvious and derived from how

The Movie

has facilitated the demise of

The Theatre

as the 'home' of acting....and how

The Internet & Social Media

are slowly

altering Movie & TV World

&

reshaping how American Intimacy occurs.

A few thoughts about theatre....

Theatre in America, as you know, has been nationally marginalized.

What's Going On & What's Next

Its metaphor is that of a Beached Whale surrounded by devotees who patiently and lovingly circle with candles, watching and waiting, nurturing and feeding it with plays, productions, loyalty, love, and hopes.

When theatre responds, the devotees rejoice and continue to participate in what's left: Regional Theatre in slow atrophy, small Urban Theatre struggling, alt. theatre busy, and Community Theatre doing what it does.

Facts:

- There's no pot of pay-fame *gold* at the end of the Theatre Rainbow….*unless* you love to act in an environment where the fun of make-believe, the pleasure of language, and the intimacy of ensemble effort are all coordinated for the joy of story-telling with others in continuity, night after night. That's the spiritual gold of working in theatre.

- What's left of live theatre today that anyone really knows about is Vegas, strip joints, music concerts, churches, clubs, media coverage of daily living, and the longest running, costliest extravaganza in American history: Political Antics in Washington.

The Happy Castle

+ All of this will continue until America has a stroke.

So....

For the young actor/actress, it's always a personal choice to go for the gold of your affinity on a playground other than Hollywood or New York....or Chicago or Minneapolis or Seattle....or a little bit of San Francisco and Atlanta. After that, it's theatre hinterlands.

Does it really matter that the Modern American Actor is The Known Actor?

Of course.

And no, of course not.

The 'of course' side is what this book is partly about—the inseparable union of Acting & America and why America invented its gods and goddesses of secular holiness.

The 'of course not' side is: follow your dream the way you like to do it or can do it so you can keep on doing it.

If you're not interested in fame, then go local instead of trying to go national.

There is a hierarchy to American Acting....

The Strata:

In film—
Living Legends
A-List
Really Respected Working Actors and Actresses
Really Respected Support Actors and Actresses
Brief Stars
Voice Over Work & Commercials
Here & There Gigs Actors and Actresses
Bit Players
Extras
Those in Theatre
Older Actors and Actresses Still Available
The Unknowns
It's Over
    &
In television—
Lead Television Actors and Actresses
Support Television Actors and Actresses
A Few Here & There Gigs Actors and Actresses
Holding On Actors and Actresses
Those in Theatre
Little To No Voice Over Work
Fewer Commercials
Extras

No Longer Needed
It Never Really Happened
It's Over

Question: *is* there an evolving style of American Acting today?

Yes, in film and television....

Overall, it's becoming very intimate and imitative, cadenced, intense, determined, strong and strongly patterned, often cluttered, repetitive, and narrowed to less and less language.

This can be frustrating for the actor/actress wanting to and able to do more.

What's going on today influences aspiring actors to become what they see.

Yet, within the evolving cultural constraints placed on TMAA, there are numerous actors/actresses able to make a gallon of substance from a thimble of content.

Consider:

Is America maturing?

Sure. But for now, America is a perplexed and wayward 17 year-old trying to learn how to deal with desire, fun, sex, money, weapons, things, thinking, time, responsibility, denial, true facts, actual love, the lure of the possible, arrogance, the future, and how to drive better

BUT

Kid America's first vehicle *is an 18-wheeler with a full American Load.* That means Kid America has taken the keys and, without training, gotten on the Interstate with all kinds of weather promised....and learned gears on-the-fly.

If a problem develops, there's a Driver Manual in the glove box. Read it while driving, guard your wallet, don't take any shit, don't have an accident, and hope you make it. Drive hard, no speed limit, take your chances, get away with as much as you can, and get to your destination; just *do it,* no whining....and be ready for long stretches with lotsa unpredictables and little rest.

It just doesn't seem that way.

Within all that cultural drama:

The importance of TMAA is to be glue, teacher, guide, and mini-divinity: TMAA are the hod carriers, the ones who help us build and secure our personal bunkers....show by show, movie by movie, channel by channel, app by app, series by series, sequel by sequel, concert by concert.

But…where's it all going, this American Acting Phenomenon? It's going on and on that's for sure. The Modern American Actor will continue to serve the….

Americological Need-Facts:

- Americans need melodrama *Violence* to help assuage anxiety about dying.
- Americans need *Laughter* to enjoy living and to cope with anxiety.
- Americans need *Reassurance* that legal and medical conditions will be really tended to.
- Americans need *Intimacy* to help restore diminished, absent, or lost love, community, and traditions.
- Americans need *Guidance* and encouragement related to hopes and dreams.
- Americans need *Reinforcement* of cherished beliefs.
- Americans need *Protection* from intrusion, invasion, and losses of control.
- Americans need *Images* for greater personal identity and the continuity of personal effort.
- Americans need *Revitalization* of time through, fun, things, and watching.

- Americans need some form of valid authority.
- Americans need *Respite*.

TMAA, entertainment, and gadgets largely do that for Americans.

So, as stated....

It's clear that the evolving style of American Acting is continuing to mirror America's increasing preference for more voyeuristic drama and less emotionally complex, personal drama.

That means American acting is becoming *narrow-fied* into technological expansions of thematic simplicities to match consumer preferences.

The simplicities are melodramatically and mythically *intensified* for maximum audience involvement, easy audience access, and profit.

All of this change demands that TMAA adapt with skills that integrate self, silence, and sparse dialogue to serve America's demand for Dramatic Cool and Dramatic Strong, male and female.

Along with that change, there's an overall reduction in the quality of written relationships....they're increasingly abbreviated distortions that secure immature ways of dealing with conflict, confrontation, resolutions, sex, and the facts of deeper love.

TMAA is not asked to act as humans but as behavior-type humans fulfilling what audiences want and expect to see in very particular, uncomplicated ways—not too serious, but always intense and, in the end, predictably reassuring.

That means:

Many American Movies will continue to become more melodramatically superficial: shorthand, calculated versions of actual drama....

&

Human intimacies will continue to be diminished by special-effecting and animating everything imaginatively possible so the journey from reality to fantasy-reality has more frosting, more innocence, more gratification, more fascinations, and more translocations that are still 'magical' but less and less complex.

However, a few persons will always emphasize humanity in what they make for those who want that....and this is where the playwright and independent thinker-writer-filmmaker more directly interested in the qualities of love and the complexities of the human predicament/situation will be able to answer the call, the thirst, the need....and find the best actors/actresses.

Summary:

- TMAA is becoming The Artistic Butler.
- Facts are becoming less important than opinions, emotionally driven beliefs, and preferences.
- Truth today is a soccer ball endlessly kicked around by amateurs.
- The kinds of dramatic experiences American movies are developing will continue to be based on hyperbolic dramatizations of themes requiring the continuous presence of strength, bravery, heroism, revenge, justice, romantic love, triumph, fun, sex, laughter, cool, and win

   in sharp contrast to but including

  worry, anxiety, distrust, pain, mortality, morality, and all forms of conclusive disaster and suffering in the areas of money, social issues, marriage, sex, race, politics, leadership, greed, trust, war, stability, dreams, and mature love.

- The evolving style of acting that serves these American demands will, therefore, continue to be centered on being a strong performer even in evil roles or roles of weakness....

Be strong.
Make your mark.
Stand out.

So....

The bottom line for TMAA is: be *effective* and keep working
&
Sensitive, deeply human roles will be fewer
&
There will be fewer screenwriters able to write great dramatic roles
&
Fewer directors will be fully able to guide the drama of great writing, great actors/actresses.

The meaning of great will be revised further to match a changing vision of what great writing is, what great directing is, what great acting is, what great thinking is, and what great loving is.

Additional summary facts:

- ✦ America is the most envied culture in all the world because America is the Guardian of The Possible—it's The Happy Castle.
- ✦ Lovers of dreams all around the world somehow wish to make a pilgrimage to this country. Those

who can't travel actually do it symbolically: they buy American Clothing and goods, copy Americans, see American Movies and listen to American Singers, and in varying ways adore TMAA.

- Acting will follow the shifts of commerce, and The Internet will become even more of a personal resource for watching *everything* as it happens.
- Passive arousal will increase.
- Movies will be present but they, like letter writing, books, phone conversations, the arts, and face-to-face meetings, will be absorbed into the broader cultural shifts of increased Autopia.
- Older actors/actresses/celebrities and personalities will be forgotten quicker and the younger ones—the new ones—will struggle for a lasting niche in the evolving structures of entertainment.
- Theatre will invent more use of the Internet.
- TMAA generally will have more opportunities to work but for less money.
- On-line Actor Training Programs will develop more completely.
- The Ubiquitous Lens will further define American culture.
- There will always be stars living in the Happy Castle.

Side note:

Once in a while I take photos from the front porch.
One spring afternoon I looked around.
Baldy spoke to me:

'Study clouds. Take photos of them. Study the photos. Then study the blue and the light. Then reflect on sun and light. And when night brings stars, dazzling and dancing, study them and reflect on darkness as pure light un-actualized. Then see how long you can look at stars and darkness before you lower your gaze and look around at things of earth, of your world, and inside all of that. Then try to find everything outside of you inside of you—the sun and blue, clouds and clear, night and stars, and the pure black as pure light, dazzling and dancing as stars; and find things of the earth in you that matter, your symbols. Then find me in you. I am and am not what I seem to be'.

Baldy told me to write about that in this book. So I have.

I listened because, as you know, when a mountain talks, particularly on very cold days, all white with snow, all isolated from clock time, beneath blue and clouds, sun and starry, starry nights....when a mountain talks, you automatically listen because there is no other voice in your wilderness to tell you about your wilderness.

So, if ever you live alone and isolated for more than a few days….live with all the seasons talking and telling, instructing, and waiting for you….if you ever do that, maybe you'll also hear nature talk, and you'll listen too….and discover there are two choices: cry from joy and mystery or split and go far away from your wilderness.

But know this, the wilderness you leave is the one that's always waiting to meet you so you can know you most accurately and completely.

Listening to a mountain talk is easy because a mountain is connected to everything.

I learned that.

Listening to a rabbit is different.

* * *

A personal note, a couple of memories:

About two hundred years ago

I saw westerns and other movies at the Cody Theatre owned by a quiet, round man. Earl. Next to the theatre was Old Man Henderson's small concession business, The Fountain, where, from age five through eighteen, I, like so many kids before and following my departure from Cody, bought treats from the quiet,

The Happy Castle

patient, tall, thin, bald man and took 'em into the movie where stories magically *moved*.

The magic that didn't move was land and on Cody Library's bookshelves. A few of those shelves held very old photos from around the world. I'd slip them one by one into a hand-held, wooden holder with optics that magnified the images and made what I saw more intimate: immediate and actual.

In addition to looking at photos, I'd walk between shelves and touch….*the books*. I tried to read ones I couldn't understand. They often were thick and full like big plates of food, and there was a lot of 'em. So I read, read what I could, filled up week after week.

This was

Before television arrived in Cody….a time when:

- ✦ Refrigerators were just becoming household items and washing machines were replacing 'wash day' and rinsing tubs, and telephone service was a live operator in a line of ladies sitting at a switchboard in the Telephone Office on 'main street'. Just say three numbers and one of the ladies would pull and push round plugs from and into color-coded circuitry. Magically, the number would ring.
- ✦ Ice for the icebox was delivered by Jock Wylie.

- Had to wring chickens' necks....so they could be gutted, plucked, and cooked.
- Hunted and took carcasses to the slaughterhouse to be cut and ground into meat, leftover bones for the dogs.
- Hauled and split wood for the fireplace, not knowing the world beyond Wyoming, but dreaming about it....while searching for myself among all the possibilities and kid puzzlements slowly causing a vague but strong desire to learn about the word God.

Then....

....at the Cody Theatre I, a teenager in full-blown teenage wondrousness-confusion, saw Brando....then James Dean. Paul Newman....others.

A dream was born.

I was in deep need, saddled with all the normal tensions of adolescence and the perverse, destructive craziness called my parents. And this was the fifties, a time for juvenile delinquency, the mini-rebellion of youth that would mature in the sixties.

I wanted to *act* my pain, my longing, my needs.

I wanted to break out of me so I could somehow *be* me. That's all I felt because I couldn't really think about acting in any other way—pure excitement, pure lure.

The Happy Castle

I was searching for something to put substance to my name, to my 'life' so I could develop a valid signature that felt like mine.

I had to be an actor.

So I dreamed more, all the way *into* a dream that took me half way around the world, up and down—

I rode heaven bareback....the hardest way to ride hard.

Ten years later, that unalterable pursuit of becoming one of the world's best actors ended.

I had changed.

Did I really want to be an actor?

Yes.

Until I hit no.

Hit it in the actual....and....once again there was that familiar, painfully demanding *void*, a state of raw self-ignorance and self-collision, which meant: time to seek, time to grow, time to discover.

I didn't have the words but I felt the pressure. In my slang....

I had to ride again, only this time find a saddle, bridle, and map. Not bareback.

Heaven had to be more than a dream....without losing the dream. Wasn't easy.

I look back at all that and understand the beautiful fullness of....

A metaphor when I was 22 years old....

....it occurred one night on the top deck of the Castel Felice....mid-Atlantic, in the height of a storm that fascinated me once again into the drama of *storm, wind,* and *darkness*. I wanted to be in it all, all the way in... *in the heart of it all,* in the middle of something *true*. I wanted that engagement, the adventure of *entering*.

I'd done it before, naked in an isolated Wyoming lake at midnight during a rain storm. But that was nothing compared to what I was seeing from the top deck.

So I went for it:

Climbed over protective barriers, walked unsteadily but quickly and nimbly toward the prow where I held on to an upright steel rod, looped my belt around the metal, and notched it....just before the *ship* dipped deeply into a dark maw, an empty blackness that seemed quiet beyond silence. But only for a second. Then the mighty downward thrust became an equally strong upward, *loud* drive that carried my heart, desire, and youth toward stars I could not see, all in place, secure, beyond earthly turbulence.

Once again, I was riding like I'd ridden horses....
Wave after wave....

I could have been bucked off, thrown into the Atlantic.

The Happy Castle

I could have died.

The Captain bright-lighted me from the bridge and with a speaker *commanded* in heavily accented, broken English that I return to safety.

Tricky. Had to undo my belt and turn before the slow dip began....so I *scurried*....the Happy Castle rose....I frantically searched for something to keep me from sliding into anything metal....or just going overboard....climbed the nearest barriers....could feel the ship begin to tilt quickly downward so I stopped, held a metal rail....I mean I *really held on:* arms, legs, and spirit. The wave seemed larger than previous ones because I couldn't *see it,* couldn't time it, and had no control over anything but my grip. It pounded, washed over me....so loud....a few seconds later, in the powerful rush-pull of after-water, I deeply 'saw' and truly understood *again*—I mean for deep actual—that I *could have died*.

I smiled, jubilant....but sober.

Wasn't my first encounter with dying and it wouldn't be the last, but that night the fact penetrated all the way to true because I was older.

I got it. But....

I was on my way to Europe to make my first big dream come true!

What's Going On & What's Next

I didn't know that I was really asking the big questions of age 22: Who am I? and What am I doing? and Where am I going? I was just *going*, doing it.

I didn't know those questions would persist for nearly ten more years.

All I had were the small answers:

I'm Jim Wilson and I'm going to Europe on a risk, a dream, and a dime. And I have to live. Make it.

Had I turned to 'acting' as *the* answer?

Of course.

Years later, I learned it was not the answer *except for that time*.

I couldn't understand the symbolic aspect of my quest: I needed bigger answers.

The bigger answers were in the mail. I had to wait a few more years for delivery.

When I finally opened the mail at around thirty, the info was brief, concise, and unambiguous:

- I'd wanted liberty from pain, confusion, and my parents.
- I'd seen acting as the promise of that liberation.
- I'd wanted to be me. I thought acting would provide that.
- It did and it didn't.
- I'd wanted to belong.

✦ I was saddling up for another dream: find me, be me, stay me.

Back then I didn't know—

That anyone who plays authentically for a lifetime, irrespective of formal education, will discover 'truths' because those 'truths' are manifest as greater and greater meanings inherent *only* in the journey of playing to learn them.

I didn't know meanings must be discovered rather than taught because meanings can't be taught. They can only be introduced and aroused.

I didn't know that to discover meanings, a person must be guided by the map of personal affinity.

I didn't know I would learn that play is worship, play is prayer, and play is action that translates the abstract into the concrete—it actualizes and reveals meanings essential for functioning as 'human'.

I didn't know play is the ultimate human cool and it's the only way you can become wealthy and learn to share love deeply.

I didn't know I would learn how play fulfills and reinforces the beauty of truth and the truth of beauty because it unites and binds; it secures the deepest considerations of what is loosely called 'faith'.

I didn't know I would learn how playing is the only way we can, like flowers, arch toward the sun....and join it....like little kids do.

What does arching mean?....it means:

Play is the only fortress no philosophy/religion/theology can match or any ideology defeat because the essence of play is spirit.

Therefore, play is the core, the heart of freedom.

And it's also the voice of love uniting humans to *being* and, therefore, to each other.

My daughters and students taught me about that.

Now my grandchildren, nature, animals, friends, food, tiny pleasures, challenges, and time are my tutors.

I've learned:

✦ The best practitioners in all fields honor play because they, in their respective areas of expertise, can excel only through *living* toward the good they can do, by *playing* in a chosen field filled with who they are, discovering all that's there, and, finally, sharing the harvest.

Without doing this, no 'player' can be great because....

The Happy Castle

- Human greatness is always related to authenticity, goodness, and the pursuit of excellence made possible through discovery. Period.
- Making good decisions, like all great art (including the art of living), is in the details.

At 21 I didn't know any of that. But I felt it, sensed it.

At 27 I knew some of that.

At 47 I was starting to get it.

At 74 I get it fully. I get the *now* really well because I'm closer to time than ever before and I'm still riding, still truckin'.

At this age, surrounded now by melting snow, open land, wide sky blue, Baldy nearby, and moisture's promise to make land luxuriously green for a while, I know what I know....as a veteran warrior for the good, as a champion for love, and as a dreamer still standing, willing to learn more.

That's partly why my heart leaps

When I see sun melt night to dawn to deep blue....

When I feel my body-life respond to *life*...

When I eat really good food that's really good for me....

When I sit naked on a chair near the laundry room and feel sun warm me....

When I dream....

When I share time with friends and family....

When I Skype my grandson, Maverick, and granddaughters, Vivienne Rose and Maisie Rae.

When I haul ass in my truck....I love trucks....

I'm glad I can leap, that I love to leap, that I always did love to leap....
    &
That's why
I leapt all the way from my theres and heres to every this and that, and all the way to this Wyoming again....yeah:

I leapt into time.

I leapt into college, I leapt into Europe, into studying, living, struggling, and searching.

I leapt into beds.

I leapt into career.

I leapt into marriage.

I leapt into more adventure

I leapt into unforeseeable mistakes.

I leapt into trucks and hotrods.

I leapt into horses.

I leapt into all seasons and into fatherhood, and that leap helped me leap into the drive to love when love seemed impossible.

The Happy Castle

I leapt into writing fifty years ago....leapt into space.

A lotta times after leaping, I stumbled, fell, got hurt, hurt others.

Didn't mean to do that. Ever.

Okay....

Back on track:

Much genius in America, as you know, is lost due to poverty and parents, ignorance and negligence, and bad forms of laziness.

Arrogance and passive disregard make children into pennies....

Which translates as the following cruel American facts:

- Cost overwhelmingly determines the direction of American decisions about American people. Money over the living. That means
- The privilege of The Privileged is the privilege to preserve privileges. The Privileged usually do just that, no matter what.
- A lot of Americans want to join The Privileged. The only way to do that is through more money. That's why....
- America will never fail financially.

- These facts are present in every aspect of The American Privileged—from the heavily attended mega-churches to all schools that homogenize the young into the negative ethics of cultural conformity, and to the Slaughter Offices of many American Politicians.

Money's important, yes, and it needs to be taken seriously....
>   but

To make it the *center of faith*—that has happened. We all know it. We see it every day.

And, as you also know:

- Bias and ignorance aren't a good combo; they're the basis of 'profane'.

What is 'profane'?
It's not plain old cursing, swearing.

It's the actuality of diminished regard for love.

Jack the rabbit is never profane.
No animal or natural environment is profane.
Only humans are stubbornly profane.

About ignorance and the little ones:

The deepest lessons for the young in schools are *within truly good teachers* of the young.

The lessons the young see first are *in* a teacher's eyes when first *seeing each student* and remembering each child's name.

The lessons the young hear first are *in* a teacher's tone of voice and, therefore, *in* the words a teacher says.

Because

The deepest lessons for the young are contained *in* the teacher's heart. Always.

That's what wee ones learn to trust.

So....

How a really good teacher includes any student is always with eyes revealing a loving heart that shapes words, and how instruction unites student and teacher in the task of learning....

because the teacher knows how to teach individuals, not classes

because

that's how the best learning occurs.

Which brings to mind....

When I wrote earlier in this book that drama is the intensification of human experience, I went on to write that there are two major forms, artistic and non-artistic. And I mentioned there's a third form of drama I'd address later.

That later is now.

The third form is *spiritual drama*—the *meanings* in all artistic and non-artistic drama.

That means:

Spiritual drama is an inescapable fact of living, expressed in every human thought and effort, and in every human encounter.

Consider:

- Spiritual drama is the omnipresence of love, even in love's absence. It is *the* most powerful and influential aspect of living. This assertion presumes that love is not narrowly defined as (or confined to) feeling.
- Great art, great living, and genuine kindness are shields and prayers, weapons and havens, and our affirmations of self, others, meanings, and 'life'.
- It's a well-known fact that we cannot create, we can only recombine that which already exists and call our efforts creative of the new that feels like 'creation'.

Creation is a white-hot word many folks misunderstand because of extreme bias and intractable ignorance.

- The ineradicable, inexplicable, and unalterable bottom line absolute that can be used to validate any discussion of creation is: meanings and divinity are concentrated synonyms for the mysterious depth of the word 'one'.

The spiritual definition/denotation/implication of the word 'one' is: all is.

All is, if reflected upon, rhymes with total interrelatedness, which is summarized by the word love.

Otherwise, arrogance, ignorance, and negligence will continue to separate meanings, divinity, and persons preferentially—arbitrarily. This fact is the dominant aspect of all actions in the domain of profane and, therefore, it's also the basis for what the word secular actually means and what religions are becoming....

Isolated identity clubs.

So....

The challenge is: how to keep living from fragmenting into profane—diminished regard for love.

When we break love, what is it we are doing?

The only fix-it is greater meanings embraced and applied. That requires strength, courage, patience, labor, deep honesty, motivation, and growth.

Great artistry in any field reveals that because great art and great persons move us, touch us right where the good and the beauty live and intersect in us. And we feel, in that beauteous moment when good and beauty touch us, the depth of the word 'healing'.

That means:

Great artistry in any field activates what we call 'truth' as love. I'm not writing about tacky love, cheap love or love for a dime or emaciated love or sentimental love felt as deep love, or harsh force-love or dumb love, etc.

None of that holds anything together except personal neurosis.

Love is made of love to bind love so love grows humans into the fullness of being truly in—inside—love.

That's why love fascinates us, and why we all long for it, often miss it, and regularly forget to do it as a way of living: we forget to be that beauty for self, another human, and for children, animals, and the environment extending into space.

Spiritual drama.

Humbly, I believe....

Living depends on the will to love. It's a choice many folks never really make with any depth or duration.

The will to love signifies an inherent quest for what we most naturally are—good.

We say life is good. Our task, as stated, is to match the beauty of life by how we live toward, for, and into the good.

Art does not <u>explain</u> any of this

because

Art is humanity in code form.

We feel the code whenever we encounter art in our humanity, in the humanity of others, in wee ones, in what we or others make or give for the good, and in kindness given or received.

An artist, any kind of artist, always feels the code simply by trying to translate it through the effort to 'make' the good happen.

A great artist gets more of the whole code and shares it more completely through a superior use of 'Artistic Braille'—meanings we can sense and feel in their works: experience.

Lesser art presents less of the code. Less experience, less meaning.

So….

Consider:

Few persons are great in any field.

All persons can do greatness as genuine kindness.

Greatness can't be sought or bought.

Great persons and artists will tell you that. Great pretenders will tell you something else.

- Persons genuinely inspired to become artists do not *aspire* to become artists. They identify intimately with their passionate involvement as *endeavor:* to learn, discover, elucidate, illuminate, and express through the *code* what they (we) carry inside.

As stated, the code causes the desire, the need, and the demand to *make:* somehow translate the code—engage it, then embrace it through endeavor and sharing what is made.

- Either you are timelessly smitten by an activity that has 'grasped your being' because it's genuinely in you to do or you're romantically smitten by an activity that grabbed your longing to be grabbed—to matter.

So:

- Love what you do….it actualizes you while you actualize 'it'.
- The extent you can be actualized by what you do, give, and receive—the good—becomes the meaning and purpose of living and the measure of what you become.

- ✦ If you romance living, you'll never 'make love' to living.
- ✦ If you do not make love to living, you'll court shallowness that can easily go south into bitterness, meanness, and destructiveness that can easily turn you into hardness that can easily become a lock against love, loving, and yourself.

This happens often in little ways, big ways. And lotsa folks often try to pick the lock with emotional and/or physical violence, or money or denial or control.

- ✦ TMAA is hired primarily to act all that drama.
- ✦ The only categories of persons not subject to overt criticism for 'playing too much' are The Modern American Actor, the ultra-conservative, and children.

Why?

TMAA is indispensable, irreplaceable, and therefore essential for shifting American Culture Norms.

The ultra-conservative is a reminder of what to avoid becoming.

The Actor/Actress play hard.

Ultra-conservatives hardly play because playing is hard.

The child is divine.

But is The Actor/Actress taken seriously as a *person?*

The surface perception is they're *not* persons. They're actors and actresses, fascinating and wonderful, to be watched through The Lens and stared at in public because they've come from The Happy Castle into the daily world, our world....for a moment....*as* persons.

Aspiring actors/actresses camp with dreams near The Castle.

Acting teachers know this hope all too well.

Acting teachers also know many are called, few chosen, fewer last.

Nevertheless....

Thousands of young folks annually begin their reach for the stars. They pursue, sustain, and wait. They adapt. Time passes. Those who continue to mature and respond to changing personal facts still find ways to *play.* That alone is a self-beauty worth preserving because of how it manifests in relationships, family, the sacredness of a child, and the preservation of authenticity and sanctity.

Additional facts:

+ All great entrepreneurs fly into profit, then maybe into some philanthropy.

The Happy Castle

- All great engineers fly ideas into tangible structures.
- All great astronomers, cosmologists, and astrophysicists fly into the universe, driven by pure wonder and all the possibilities in starry, starry night.
- All great athletes learn to fly and train to fly higher, better.
- All deep humanitarians soar into love and stay there.
- All great leaders seek the sun.
- All babies fly the smile.
- All great parents learn how to fly again for the continuity of a child's continued smiling flights.
- All great poets and writers, artists and actors, actresses, singers, scientists, caregivers and nurses, environmentalists, activists, kind persons, animal lovers, parents, musicians, and leaders fly us....so when we're lost, we know what to remember, appreciate, value, and preserve.
- Great women teach us how to love. They are the womb of all play.

I told my daughters:

Do what you love, love what you do, and do it full-on to learn how to include and coordinate the essentials, aka No Clutter.

I bored them further by saying:

To achieve No Clutter requires hardcore training. That means humbly remain in pursuit of learning to live and living to learn so you can learn to love and love to learn.

That's how self-help, help-self works.

Easy to say.

Final thoughts on teaching acting:

If *pedagogy* suggests the art or science or profession of teaching, then what does pedagogy *actually* mean in the actual world of teaching the young the elusive experience called acting?

It means very little because in daily living anyone who has a background in acting can become a teacher with a philosophy or method or theory or approach reflecting what impressed the actor/actress before he/she decided to be a teacher.

So….

Personal experiences, one's teachers, books written by actors who became teachers, the content of living, some common sense, and the content of one's personal psychology become the basis for formulating the 'how to' of teaching.

However,

That often tends to distort the focus and mission of teaching away from the holiness of truly valid instruction.

But

For those who develop the art of teaching, their authenticity is always wonderful to observe.

But

When a teacher of acting is minimally creative, pedagogy can become tenaciously and/or lopsidedly focused on theory, glossary (action, objectives, goals, wants, etc.), discussion, analytical inquiries, intense demands, narrow emphases, etc.

Fact:

There can be no 'science' to the teaching of acting because there *can't* be any science to the actualities of creativity: creativity is qualitative before it's quantitative.

But teaching *can and should* manifest the *artistry of guidance*.

That fact presupposes a teacher knows how to create an environment that attracts students *appropriately* to the activity of *any* class anywhere in any field of study and, therefore, to any kind of acting class: voice, movement, directing, acting, design, lighting, production, dialects, improvisation, script, singing, dance, and acting.

They're *all* acting classes, each with an emphasis that requires masterful, invisible guidance for learning, confidence, artistic independence, and the creative *integration of all pertinent emphases.*

Then a student can genuinely explore into the content of any class and identify with the activity in ways that reveal the interdependency of all emphases. From that, learning can become more cohesively valid and more creatively progressive toward artistry in any area of any field.

This journey takes time.

The most useful, generalized definition of pedagogy for a teacher is to gently talk to the mirror and say: 'Get out of the way of the student. Figure out completely what that means and what teaching means. Then teach better. Learn more'.

The task is demanding; it takes a lot of maturity, informational expertise, humility, humor, flexibility, the willingness to modify cherished approaches to teaching: alter self….grow as a person and as a teacher.

Any good teacher serves the student wholly and individually as much as the learning context permits.

Thousands of teachers and administrators in all educational institutions are guilty of neglecting that responsibility.

That means:

Is teaching a job or an opportunity to *work?*

To appreciate the answer to that question requires that a teacher learns to teach to learn how to teach better so students can learn without noticing the teaching.

Side note:

As stated, I taught for a long time.

Sat in many meetings centered on a real slippery topic.

Lost interest while colleagues tried to hammer a favored view of a topic into place with such intensity that I chose a different view—the one beyond the window.

The topic was methodology.

I'm too much of a little kid to engage sincerely for long in that kind of endless, often biased, speculative, anecdotally defended involvement.

When my opinion was sought or I spoke, I could only offer nuts and bolts correlations of facts and effort to keep structure, substance, and relevancy in the Student Zone—what *today's* students needed to learn and how they could best learn it from us by teaching *us* how to teach them by changing a curriculum, reorganizing syllabi, altering assignments, and growing as teachers.

That said....

Every acting class I've taught anywhere (after I began to learn how to teach) was always introduced with a statement of two concerns:

'Make it believable and do it your way. Then make sure what you learn is valid. Put me on the spot and get your money's worth'. I added 'We can build on all that unless you get in the way of yourself somehow or you discover your affinity for this dream is less than you thought it was and not enough for you to keep on truckin'. Then change out and find out what's next for you. But until you grow into greater self-clarity about who you are and what acting is, keep it honest, keep it real, keep it playful, and stay open. Play again and again and do it with increasing responsibility so the dream that can come true will come true because it will evolve you, and from that you will know if it's the dream you're supposed to be dreaming'.

I never had a pedagogy or much methodology other than 'We start with the basics and what you can do now, then expand your capability without losing the pleasure of playing. I'll take you as far as you want to go. It's up to you'.

Not bragging. I meant it. Still do.

Flipside—inappropriate emphases:

- Coercive methods, the Boot Camp Drill Instructor Abuse Technique, or any other instructional mode that is demeaning, intimidating, petty, controlling, analytically abusive, argumentative, off-centered, and disrespectful.
- Blimpy inflations of voice, movement, and text analysis.
- Too much talk, not enough do.
- Disguised lay-psychotherapy.
- *Theory* and Glossary emphases instead of simple, accurate, uncluttered guidance that is purely valid.

Student routes to employment:

Theatre classes
A Degree in Theatre
Graduate Study in Theatre
The Professional Schools
The Workshop Route

Know Someone
Be discovered
Wing It
Luck

So....

If you're dreaming the dream you should be dreaming, continue to learn. Study/train creatively.

Do what you have to do to keep the dream alive.... this includes finding ways to improve your acting.

Do this....

In spite of

The pressures of getting older.

But how, without some success in acting, some validation other than local theatre, student films, making a reel, inventing and producing your own stuff, attending an acting workshop, seeing film after film and tv program after program where some of your friends are working but not *you*—how do you put all that together and say 'I'm doing it?' How do you handle the collision of a dream with the feeling of being left out?

The best way is:

With deep honesty and equal action....

Do it. Keep learning.

So, the question....

What can an aspiring actor <u>do</u> alone to improve?

The answer might not seem valid. It's based on the heart of human living and, therefore, acting.

The answer is language.

If you're talented, increased long-term emphasis on language will ultimately polish your uncut self-gem.

You don't *read* language.

You *live with it* because you can already read.

You get to know it, how it lives.

You woo it so you can join it, so you can surrender to what it *is* in you until you can express what it is *through* you.

You do this until language can finally be spoken by you and love you back freely with more insights for greater completion—artistry.

That process always leads you into the writer's code, the Artistic Braille, for expressing substance rather than content: living rather than calculating and assembling....craft versus portrait, artistry versus entertainment.

So....

You

Fully humanize all rehearsals openly wherever you play-work—alone, with a friend, or in rehearsals of any kind.

And you

Check out how to do that. That means, through reading aloud and talking to yourself like a kid on a treasure hunt; do all this while seated and/or moving....or going silent, feeling stumped, but always excited by the maybe of the quest.

And you

Check out how great poets combine structure, phonemes, religion, meanings, philosophy, and human experience.

Check out how great playwrights imbue language with human experience.

Check out how great screenwriters shape scenes and language to imbue both with story and human experience.

Check out how great actors do their thing.

Check out great scenes, rewind, get the script on paper, and see what actors/actresses started with and what they did with it because of what it did with them. Then you try it without imitating—do it your way, figure out what that truly is, and make it believable on the playwright's or screenwriter's terms.

Always reach for the best you can do. And do it with a sense of humor, a sense of playing around and looking for creative answers so you can *learn* to trust answers you determine are accurate, even though you may feel blind half the time. Trust that sight improves. Stay open to seeing the more.

If you are truly talented and you woo language to let it teach you, *you will learn.*
&
If you can study with a qualified teacher who can guide your thinking and efforts in all areas, you will learn.
&
If you keep on learning, growing, you will be noticed.

You will work. There's always a way.

The goal of these comments is to encourage you to explore 'the possible' in you and in a writer's language so you can learn *how* to portray rather than perform.

That means learn to perform a portrayal.

Fact:

All of this may seem petty, idealistic, lecturey, tedious, and, ultimately, irrelevant. It's not. Unless you believe it's not relevant for you.

I'll stop.
Only a few pages left….time to focus on:

Jack

Every time I hitch-hiked in America and Europe I remember wondering, what's up ahead?.... remember the dramatic immediacy of standing on the *road*....small canvas bag, cool jacket, bright eyes, willing heart, and sunny excitement for the next wherever as part of getting beyond where I stood....arm rolling upward, thumb high in sync with a passing vehicle.... then turn and watch a driver's decision to slow and pull over or disappear on down the road....

That was then.
Different thumb-up now.
Different kind of ride....
Yeah....a *different* stretch of highway somewhere between mountains and big water, between thousands of the this and that of a lifetime....I see peaks and water, all my here of there, there of there, clarity about all this of that and that of this, and I see this

here....a bright now of human twilight, on a rural cabin, and I see this book instead of a small, canvas bag....yeah, I still have some cool jackets, more jeans, solid trucks.

    &

I'm still standing, wondering, reflecting, remembering, still looking forward....but it's always thumb up....and let's do it.

Jack's told me a lot at different times, different seasons, early and late, in light and in the dark...

One other night I got pissed off that I'd shoveled snow *twice in one day*....but at 11 p.m., another four inches....I went out, shoveled hard *again*—porch light on—and sang loud, angrily, happily defiant, frustrated, determined; sang my way down the dark lane in bright moonlight....sang 'On The Wings of A Snow White Dove'....walked back, and there by the porch fence, Jack was watching me. We stared.

This is how I met Jack:

He's wild.

Lives beneath old, leftover tin leaning against the garage to prevent foundation damage from heavy snow and drip-ice that forms a baby glacier....doesn't melt until April.

He has a lady. I call her Bunny.

Jack

I juice vegetables, offer the pulp to Jack and Bunny....put it out by the fence, near the front porch.

And then one day, once upon a time, this—this happened:

A cool May afternoon a few years ago....walked outside. Jack was ten feet away, eating pulp and watching me with a dark inscrutable eye, ears twitching from thousands of years of training to avoid being killed.

He paused. 'Jack, I'm Jim. My dog's name is Lucky. Hi'.

Jack stopped chewing....'You and your dog are on my land.' Surprised, I was silent. Long stare. 'And you think my name is Jack? Rabbits don't have names.'

'Okay....'.

'Do you even know what 'rabbit' is?'

'When you put it that way, no'.

'My family goes way back. Back so far I can see stars before fur'.

'Oh'.

'What about you?'

'What about me?'

'Hard for you to be straight with a rabbit?'

'Uhhh....'.

'I can tell you everything about anything. Any animal or plant can. Even a rock. You believe that?'

'Well....I guess so'.

'But you're not sure, so you're being polite. Try me'.
'Anything?'
'What did I say? Did I say anything. Yes, I did. So ask me'.
'Anything. Okay....'.
'You think I'm kidding?'
'No, it's just that....'
'That you're not used to talking to a rabbit. And then you're not used to talking to a rabbit who can talk. And third, you're not used to the fact of an all-knowing rabbit. She's just the same. All rabbits are the same. All plants and fish and animals are the same, but you don't see all of us that way, do you? No. Because you look *at* us. You call her Bunny and think it's cute, as in bunny rabbit. It's not. There are no names except in your world. We met on that hill that's part of what you call your land...right over there where the fencepost is, where Mary put plastic flowers in barbed wire, made a wreath and hung it....there...see that spot?'
'Yes'.
'Do you know why there's only one post in the ground right there? Kinda odd, huh....one post. I know why'.
'Why?'
'There was a great goose who used to fly over this land. We met. He told me he was going to be killed by one of your group. That happened. I saw it. But three

years earlier, in 1843, one of you on horseback—you call his group Indians—brought a post, dug a hole, placed the post solidly, and attached ten feathers to it. The rocks on the ground near the post are the ones he put in place. The goose told me every ten years a feather would blow away. In your 1943 there were no more feathers. You know why? No, you don't know why. Humans don't know that much. Not really. Think about it. I'm what you call a rabbit and you're listening to me tell you about a post with ten feathers that took a hundred years to blow away. Is this real? You can't decide can you? Typical. Anyway, the answer to the post and feathers and the Indian and the goose and me….and now you, is this—this is what the goose said to me and I'm saying it to you. Want to hear it?'

'Yes'.

'The goose said: "I am grateful for the slope seeking the rising sun." That's what the goose said. You and your group call it earth….and love. This conversation will inform you that I'm an anonymous aria rabbit and you are listening to my lyrics and music, music you can't hear unless I tell you how to listen. The feathers the goose talked about….what do you think they mean? Time and air. And flight. I'm a rabbit. But I can fly too. I saw the man bring the post, place it, place the feathers, release, and fly away, straight up because he became a feathered arrow for his powerful bow made of what you call spirit. A weak word but it's the best you can do to describe what you can't understand. Can you understand what I'm telling you? No, you can't. Why did the man place ten feathers on a post and make a circle of rocks around the post?'

'Why?'

'To offer. You will understand….in time. When you learn to offer feathers for time to fly….you. Look over there near the fence. That's the one you call Bunny and those are our brood. We run together. Live together. Do you think rabbits love? I have to go. Right now. Thanks for the pulp'.

'You bet. But I didn't ask you anything'.

'You will'.

I don't have names for Jack's offspring. Maybe they don't need names.

They just ran across the yard.

It's late afternoon. Sun bright, spilling lavishly over edges of full, round clouds.

Friends have asked why I live here.

The most honest answer is to deal with unfinished love, make a home, publish books, do a little more teaching, and declare more war on myself.

I've discovered that finding a home isn't possible for any human until starry, starry night is included.

&

I've learned unfinished love is forever.

That said, I've been turning an old cabin into a house, a house into a home, and now a home into a poem. Jack understands that language. I'm glad. Maybe that's why he talked to me.

Friends have asked, "Why live alone?"
The most honest answer is to be naked in nature and my nature. Raw. In the simples.
That sounds poetic, idealistic, vague, and spiritually noble because it's all of that and more. Deeply so.
For me.

I like naked, raw, and the simples. Sometimes it hurts, hard.
I've been very naked here.
And I've learned some simples. One of them is, if I don't move, nothing moves.
Wind continually reminds me of that fact.
Wind is as simple as it gets.

I never thought about that when I was preparing for this adventure: dreaming, planning, saving, and waiting for the right time. I gambled. Almost lost the bet. Took the risk. Made it.
I bought Jack's land sight unseen and kept on plugging, kept on working and planning, trying to design

and shape living to match my needs for home, nature, and solitude that always releases crowds of thought....
So

I bought this hundred year old cabin for $400, tore it down, and moved it. Put it back up. Didn't *know* what I was doing but I knew *what* I was doing—making a dream come true. That's all I knew. That's what I do.

When I finally moved in the cabin was unfinished. Space between logs, no running water, only a toilet that flushed, electricity, and a water line connected to a pump pulling from a creek. The doors locked but critters could still get in. It's 140 miles roundtrip for good groceries and I haul my drinking water. Million dollar view north-east-west. Semi-arid except in spring....

One morning, I reached for a hat and found five newborn mice in it.

I entered the bedroom and saw a rattlesnake coiled and playing its beads near the armoire. Killed it with a shovel.

Hornets on the windows.

Flies everywhere.

Spiders—widows and others—just hangin' out.

Then came the grasshoppers. Ate every tree I planted.

Had to get the logs chinked.

Had to get the place tight against strong wind that blew dust into everything.
Had to get sinks in.
Had to make the place habitable.
Had to make it.
Had to make $ last.
Had to take the first two winters with two little space heaters.
Had to haul drinking water.
Had to get used to seasons fast.
Had to learn how to adjust to winters.
Had to think about the new way of living.
Had to learn how to adjust to no family.
Had to come to terms with my choices.
Had to keep the sun real bright.

Sometimes the gray won.
Sometimes night won.
Adjustments. Adaptations. Stymyied….
But always, git 'er done & keep on truckin'.

I've learned:
The best dreaming does make you deeply naked.
To be naked isn't romantic.
It means bereft but whole, bereft but full.
Bereft of what? Coverings.
Only humans can learn to be naked.

The Happy Castle

Nature and its creatures already are.

What does get naked mean for a human?

It means take off your culture, your history, and your name.

What's left is nakedness in the now that includes your time, your love, your lessons, your inviolable priorities, your memories, your symbols, your courage, your strength, your future, and….if you're lucky, a Baldy and a Jack.

Nakedness asks you to live.
Nakedness asks you to dream.
Nakedness asks you to love.
Nakedness asks you to give.

The older you get, the more you understand those verbs.

They make you raw. Or not.

I think that's what Jack was trying to get me to understand.

So, *why* do I live here in Wyoming?

To photograph truths.

This whole book is a series of little photos.

All the books I've written are little photos of what I know.

Jack

I'm not sure I've managed to frame the photos adequately in this book or in ways that appeal. Hope so. But that's up to you.

I know my time here in this old cabin will conclude.
I know I'm on the Castel Felice again.
This time the ocean is called land.

So *why* Wyoming?
To see the bigger picture Baldy talks from, and littler picture Jack lives in....all on wide open space and narrow space, while trying to ride heaven.

'I watch you' Jack once said. 'I listen to your thinking. That's why I decided to talk to you again'.
'Okay'.
'You went to church this morning'.
'Yes'.
'Eleven folks. A hundred and ten year old church. Lilac buds blooming against the possibility of yet another snow. You listened to the Pastor water morning's Rose with a talk about what it takes to make the Rose grow. You reflected on living in this valley. You took a leak off the porch a while ago, after you were writing what you think you're learning. Explain that learning'.
'Uhhh....I'm learning from a wild rabbit and a mountain'.

The Happy Castle

'Be glad I'm wild. What is 'wild'?'

'It's….'.

'That's pretty vague. You can do better than that. Can't you?'

'How do you know about the book?'

'You should've left the cabin where it was. But I want to go back to my question about what wild means?'

'It means living within a….'

'Not a good answer. I'm asking you again, and I'm asking why you think of me as 'rabbit'? What's the origin of the word rabbit? I'm not 'rabbit'. That's a name. I told you, in animal world there are no names, no beliefs, no concepts, no dreams. Just is. And simplicity centered on survival and procreation. That's intense and not easy. It's….wild. Wild good. Be glad you're not wild. And be sorry you're not wild'.

'Would you like to be human?'

'No. In a few minutes our conversation will never have happened except in your mind. You'll see me as 'rabbit' and you'll do what you do. Come and go, walk and talk, write and use the phone, think about a human Bunny, eat, toss me some more pulp, look around, take photos, make plans, study, and write your way up the slope to Baldy who sees the sun first. And I'll run across my land, see you, stop, stare, and hold that stare because we've connected across the divide.

Jack

And we know it. What do you really want to know most of all? What's the question you didn't ask?'

'The deep lies. What are they?'

'Interesting. They're all based on the following:

Wind is the breath of time seeking love.

Rain is the love of time seeking land.

Snow is the thought of time maturing land for the roots of trees, wild grass, flowers, and all creatures.

Light is the power of creation condensed into sun and spirit, and what you call starry, starry night.

Light is how *everything* breathes, Jim. Goodbye'.

Jack scampered. That was four months ago.

The sun has made 100 degrees, 10 days in a row. Nights cool down to around 60. I'll speak to Baldy this winter. I'll never speak to Jack again. Maybe I'll see him.

There's a last time for all encounters....

Postscript

One morning after a lightning storm and soft rain followed by big wind, I opened the front door to look at trees and see how much they'd grown overnight.
Silly me.

Looked down and saw a fragment of paper beneath a rock next to a tree stump near the old screen door. Picked it up. On it was written:

Take time....leave it breathless and smiling

Bring your granddaughters, Vivienne Rose and Maisie Rae, up for a visit. We've already met your grandson, Maverick. Nice kid.

B & J

CPSIA information can be obtained
at www.ICGtesting.com
Printed in the USA
FSHW02n1252020718
50065FS